Listen to Your LIFE

Following Your
Unique Path to
Extraordinary
Success

Listen to Your LIFE

VALORIE BURTON

WATERBROOK
PRESS

LISTEN TO YOUR LIFE
PUBLISHED BY WATERBROOK PRESS
12265 Oracle Boulevard, Suite 200
Colorado Springs, Colorado 80921
A division of Random House, Inc.

ISBN 1-57856-820-X

Library of Congress Cataloging-in-Publication Data
Burton, Valorie, 1973–
Listen to your life : following your unique path to extraordinary success / by Valorie Burton.—
1st ed.
    p. cm.
  ISBN 1-57856-820-X
  1. Success—Religious aspects—Christianity. I. Title.
BV4598.3.B87 2004
248'.4—dc22   2003025091

Printed in the United States of America
2006

10 9 8 7 6 5

To my extraordinary husband,
whose love has expanded and enriched my path beyond measure

CONTENTS

ACKNOWLEDGMENTS

I am grateful for the people whose paths cross mine and whose lives make mine richer, more joyful, and more successful. I am especially thankful to the following people for their hand in opening doors along my path that enable me to grow and to share divinely inspired wisdom with those who are open to listening. Thank you to:

My clients, readers, and audiences, for encouraging and inspiring me through your feedback, gratitude, success stories, and questions. May this book give you the tools to listen for the answers that will lead you onto your unique path to extraordinary success.

Laura Barker, editorial director at WaterBrook Press, for your enthusiasm, vision, and belief in my work—and for helping me grow as a writer.

Ginia Hairston, director of marketing and publicity at WaterBrook Press, WaterBrook publicity manager Joel Kneedler, and Ben Lauro of Pure Publicity, for the time and effort you put forth in raising the visibility of this book and spreading the word.

The entire WaterBrook team, for the spirit with which you publish this and all of your books. What a pleasure and a blessing to work with each and every one of you!

Cheryl Martin and Michelle McKinney Hammond, for passing my proposal for this book along to WaterBrook Press. God uses people to accomplish His purpose, and He clearly used you to connect me with the publisher of His choosing.

Bishop and Mrs. T. D. Jakes, for the inspiring example you set and the tremendous spiritual growth I have experienced in your church and through your ministry.

David Hale Smith, my literary agent, for your guidance and enthusiasm.

My husband, Charles Worrell. Thank you for being lovingly support-ive of my work, listening patiently as I ponder new ideas, and thoughtfully sharing ideas of your own. I love you.

And to my father, Johnny Burton Jr.; my mother, Leone Murray; my brother, Wade Murray; and all of my family and friends, for your love, support, and undying enthusiasm. I recognize that not everyone is blessed with a family as loving as you, or friends so true. I love you.

Most important, I thank God for using me as a vessel to deliver words of inspiration, truth, and personal transformation.

Listen to Your LIFE

You Are Destined for Extraordinary Success

You were born with the potential to walk an extraordinarily successful path. On this path, success is about being fulfilled in *every* area of your life, and it comes more easily and naturally because it is perfectly tailored to your unique gifts, experiences, and passion. You're connected with God, yourself, your values, and the people who matter most to you. Without hesitation, you can answer the question, Why are you here? The life you live exemplifies that purpose. All the answers you need to live that extraordinary life lie within you. But to access those answers, you must learn to listen to your life.

Listening to your life is a learned skill that can be refined and then used as a powerful tool for success. It may sound mysterious, but it simply means paying attention to the events, experiences, nudges, and passion that can steer you in the best possible direction—toward the unique path of your life's highest potential. Listening to your life involves connecting with God, yourself, and the people you encounter to get directions for finding and staying on your path. It is about being curious enough and honest enough to answer the important questions that will enable you to grow. It is about using what you hear to create a vision that pulls you forward and opening your mind to the creativity that will unlock doors and create experiences at a higher level than you have ever experienced. Listening to your life gives you both the confidence to keep walking your path even when it seems nothing is coming together the way you hoped and the tenacity to flow smoothly through the twists and turns that threaten to knock you off course. It also opens you to the rich and abundant rewards of living generously and with purpose and passion.

On the path to extraordinary success, failures along the way offer lessons that lead you to victories. The heartaches and pain cultivate the drive, compassion, and understanding you need to live at your highest potential. The mistakes, when you learn from them, give you insight that propels you forward on your journey.

Living at Your Highest Potential

Most of us live our lives at just a fraction of our potential. We peek just beyond the surface of what is possible and never look any further. To look further would mean to challenge ourselves or maybe even commit to making a major change. When dreams that stretch far beyond our comfort zone gain our attention, our subconscious interrupts with dream-shattering banter:

"You want *what?* Well, you have about a one in a million shot at that! Why don't you just be happy with what you have?"

"A career you *love?* Hah! You're lucky to have a job you *like.*"

"A business of your own? What makes you think *you* have the skills to do *that?!*"

"A joyful love life, a blissful career, family harmony, spiritual fulfillment, *and* financial freedom? Get real!"

Have you ever struggled with that kind of self-doubt? Most of us have at one time or another. As the dream-shattering banter persists, we finally give up, shut down the dreams, and tune out the possibilities.

I know because I've been there. As a life strategist, speaker, and columnist, I have coached thousands of people who have been there too. I have helped them step off the accidental path they've been wandering and step boldly onto the path of the life they were born to live. In the process, I have learned two important lessons:

1. Success is empty when you are not living your divinely appointed purpose.
2. Your unique path in life is not a mystery. If you take specific steps to listen, you will be guided directly to it.

I wrote *Listen to Your Life* to compel you to find your path, stay on it, and live the life you were created to live. I want you to stretch yourself by making radical changes through small, deliberate actions. And in the process, I want you to experience the peace and joy that come from trusting that inner voice—the voice of God—to guide you into the abundance that life has to offer. When you get to the end of your life, God doesn't want you to look back in regret at the "something more" you knew was out there but never pursued. Or to realize that you spent too much time focused on money, work, and outward appearances and not enough time creating experiences with the people you love.

My purpose in life is inspiring people to live fulfilling lives. I believe you picked up this book because you know something more awaits you. The seams of your life are bursting with possibilities, and you are ready to unleash them so you can consistently live at your highest potential.

Your highest potential is not to be confused with your highest performance level. I am not talking about adding more effort or more activities to your already busy schedule. I am talking about living a fuller, richer life with less effort, more fun, and tremendous benefits. This way of life empowers you to serve the world with your natural gifts and talents, while being compensated for doing so. It nurtures you with a cushion of abundance in every area of your life so that you have the freedom to make choices that reflect your innermost desires. And it gives you confidence that even if you fail, the fall will not be too hard to bear.

As we journey through these pages together, we will explore the principles that will lead you onto your unique path to extraordinary success—and help you stay on course. This perspective of success is focused on the "whole you." I am talking about *true* success—extraordinary success—the kind that fully expresses who you are.

How Do You Define Success?

Extraordinary success means *living with purpose* in every key area of your life, including:

- your spiritual life
- your physical health and environments
- your relationships
- your work
- your finances and resources

So often the world's role models of success are actually just stereotypes of success; they represent only a person's career or financial picture. You can be financially successful and yet not have an extraordinarily successful life. If you choose to buy into stereotypes that overemphasize career and money and de-emphasize health, fulfillment, relationships, and intimacy with God, you will find yourself pursuing a weak substitute for true success—and you'll be deeply disappointed and dissatisfied when you attain it.

Extraordinary success is unique for each of us. We must define it for ourselves. Without a definition for success, how will you know when or if you are successful? The answer is simple: You won't. However, if you fail to define success, the world will define it for you—and the world's definition may lead you to a cycle of failure, empty success, or living below your life's potential—none of which is true to your divinely ordained path.

When I headed a public relations firm, one of the most important lessons I learned was to help my clients define success before we proceeded with a project. Otherwise, we would find ourselves in the middle of a project, doing the things that would lead to success as we defined it, but not necessarily as the client defined it. Sometimes our definition would far exceed the client's. At other times the client's expectations might be less than reasonable.

For our clients to succeed and for our services to be of the most value to them, we needed a clear understanding of what they were looking for. Not only did this understanding help us reach the desired goals, but it also helped us recognize early on whether a client's definition of success was too big, too narrow, or too small.

Clearly defining what you want and by what date you want it is one of the most important steps to success. Once you are specific about what you want and when you want it, your wheels begin to turn, and you can get to work planning the success you want. When you have a definite target for which you can aim, the likelihood of success is much greater than if you declared a vague goal with no deadline in sight.

I suggest that you employ the power of the written word as you create your own unique definition of success. We will discuss this success-definition process more later, but for now, begin thinking of ways in which your view of success has been shaped—possibly even skewed—by other people in your life or by society as a whole.

Throughout this book, you'll find exercises and questions that prompt you to explore your definition of success more deeply, so you may find it very useful to keep a journal or notebook handy to record your thoughts and action plans. As you write about your life's path to success, give yourself the freedom to be open and honest. You don't have to share your thoughts and experiences with anyone else unless you want to. This is an inward journey that will ultimately manifest itself in outward success. Thank you for giving me the privilege of walking with you on your journey.

Are you ready to get started? Let's begin.

CONNECTION

Getting in Touch with God, Yourself, and Others

Trust in the LORD with all your heart,
And lean not on your own understanding;
In all your ways acknowledge Him,
And He shall direct your paths.

—PROVERBS 3:5-6

Consider for a moment the chain of events that led you to the life you are living right now.

Isn't it amazing how one thing leads to another and another until we arrive at one particular moment and place in time? Sometimes it's the place we're supposed to be, and sometimes we simply know that another path awaits us and we yearn to find it. A persistent voice whispers softly but urgently: "You're going in the wrong direction. There's a path over here with your name on it." Even if we are unaware of where our path is, God will find a way to lead us to our destiny—and *connect* us with the right people who cross our path. The key is listening to what your life is trying to tell you, following the voice of the Holy Spirit, and walking directly onto your own unique path.

CATHLEEN'S STORY

While enjoying a casual brunch with a group of inspiring women one Sunday, I asked one of them, Cathleen, how she got her start as an upscale jeweler. A fashionable and energetic woman in her early forties, Cathleen had just left a job with a cable television network to focus fully on her line of jewelry. It was a bold move, but she was clearly up for the challenge. In less than three years, she had gone from making jewelry as a hobby to creating a line of distinctive jewelry carried by Saks Fifth Avenue and exclusive boutiques around the country.

Her journey began in January 2000 on an afternoon when she just happened to be at home and tuned in to *The Oprah Winfrey Show*. Cathleen disagreed with a guest on the show who was talking about relationships, and she felt unusually compelled to log on to Oprah's Web site and fire off an e-mail expressing her thoughts. To her surprise, the next day she received a call at work from a producer at the show. They were planning to tape another program on relationships and wanted to consider Cathleen as a guest. She connected with the producer and had a friendly conversation. While chatting, they briefly stumbled onto the topic of Cathleen's favorite pastime: making jewelry. It was a hobby born of her childhood fascination with unique stones, seashells, and gems. Creating necklaces, rings, bracelets, and earrings out of precious gemstones, sterling silver, and Austrian crystals was a passion that came naturally to her—and her enthusiasm is obvious to anyone who speaks with her.

The producer ended the conversation, saying, "We'll call you back if we decide we'd like to have you on the show." A few months later, when planning a show about the importance of following your heart, the producer called and asked Cathleen to send samples of her jewelry. The samples were a hit, and they booked her for the show!

Inspired by Oprah's words of encouragement during the taping and an overwhelming response to her jewelry, Cathleen began taking the steps that led to the creation of her company, Cathleen Whitelow Jewels. She admits she never would have made the leap into entrepreneurship if things had not lined up so clearly and if she had not received the tremendous boost of confidence that came from attracting the attention of people at *The Oprah Winfrey Show* and Saks. A series of connected events led her onto her unique path in which she uses her natural talents to serve the world through her business. And it all began on an afternoon off, when she was watching television and listening to her intuition—God's inner prompting—to send an e-mail.

MAKING CONNECTIONS TO FIND YOUR PATH

Have you ever felt compelled to do something that seemed silly or inconsequential? Sometimes we receive "a divine nudge" to take a specific action because God will use that action to cause our path to cross another's at a specific moment.

It may appear to some to be luck or chance, but it isn't. These things happen every day—divinely arranged connections with people sparked by an action taken after listening to one's heart, mind, and spirit. Connection is at the core of the other six principles in this book. It is the foundation of your life—an invisible web that connects you to God, yourself, and others. And it is a vital principle for finding your unique path to success.

I call your path unique because although there are many paths you can follow, only one was uniquely designed for you. It is the path in which life, though not always easy, is divinely orchestrated and perfectly suited to your experiences, talents, and authentic desires.

The first step to finding that perfect path is connection, the process of relating and listening to God, yourself, and others. Connection empowers you to find your path, stay on it, and return to it when you stray. As you connect to your own unique experiences, purpose, and possibilities, you become aware of a sense of inner knowing or certainty that guides every key decision in your life.

Whether or not we recognize or understand it, we *all* crave connection. Even the most successful of the successful—by the world's standards—find themselves miserable, depressed, addicted to drugs or sex or shopping, or experiencing some other form of emptiness when they are disconnected from one or all of these three key relationships.

Disconnecting and Reconnecting

In my own life I have found a common thread woven through life-changing experiences of failure, confusion, frustration, and a lack of purpose. Each setback could be traced to a sense of disconnection either from my own desires and values, my relationship with God, or other people whose presence and wisdom is crucial to my well-being. At those frustrating times in my life, it has been my willingness to reconnect with who and what matter most that pulled me through.

Nearly four years after I launched my public relations firm, I felt as though my spiritual life were waning. I didn't pray as often, I was disillusioned with church, and I took very little time for myself. I found myself dreading the very work I had once dreamed of doing. I enjoyed interacting with clients and the employees who worked with me every day, but I simply wasn't excited about the work itself. I was confused by my behavior and felt guilty that perhaps I was being ungrateful. God had blessed me with a business I had asked for, and now the business felt more like a burden than a blessing.

When prospective clients would request a proposal from us to handle their public relations needs, I procrastinated. *What is wrong with me?* I wondered. *What kind of entrepreneur doesn't want more money from good clients?* I knew the answers to my questions, but I did not want to admit them to anyone, including myself. I was good at public relations, but I was not passionate about it.

Through hard work and a talent for writing, marketing, and connecting with people, my team and I had created a business we could be proud of, and we developed a reputation for being strategic, professional, and effective. In our fourth year of business, I was featured as one of the nation's rising stars in public relations by *PR Week*, a top industry publication. When another agency owner featured in the article called to congratulate me, I was disturbed to realize that I didn't share his enthusiasm for the profession. Around that time, sleeping became a struggle. For six consecutive weeks, I woke up three to five times every night, my soul restless.

I prayed that God would give me passion for my work, but He didn't. I created exciting, ambitious goals for the company, hoping they would fuel a passion in my heart. They didn't. A year and a half earlier, my purpose had been revealed to me: Through writing and speaking, I was to inspire people to live fulfilling lives. I had started down that path and had gotten a taste of how fulfilling it is to live with purpose. I had found my passion, but it didn't pay the bills. I tried writing a second book, but the words simply would not flow. Everything in my life was telling me that it was time for a new turn in my path, but I was afraid to listen. Until I turned, however, nothing I did worked the way I wanted.

When I finally admitted my fear, frustration, and confusion to myself and to God (who already knew exactly what I was feeling!), I began to make the connection I needed. I surrendered my ego, my fear of what others might think, and my fear of venturing beyond the only career I had known. I connected with myself by being honest about what I wanted despite the fact that it would require a major change in my life. I connected with God by surrendering to the direction in which He was steering me. Then, one by one, God connected me to the people who would be instrumental in my transition, including the person to whom I would sell the business. People opened doors for me to write, speak, coach, and appear as a guest as well as a host on television and radio shows.

Amazingly, each of these people was linked in some way to my public relations endeavors! The connection of events and experiences was suddenly obvious: The agency not only fulfilled an entrepreneurial dream and gave me priceless experience early in life, but it was an essential part of my unique path. I had been on the right path all along, but now it was leading me in a new direction. Listening to my life provided the clarity and confidence I needed to take the turn without looking back.

Recognizing the Difference

We have all experienced connection and disconnection on some level even if we did not know how to describe them at the time. Connection leaves you feeling clear, focused, moved to action, and full of energy. What makes you feel connected?

I feel connected when...

Disconnection, on the other hand, can leave you feeling frustrated, scattered, distant, overwhelmed, weighted down, confused, unsure, or mentally overloaded. These feelings cause you to lose your way, make poor decisions, or even give up. What triggers these reactions in you?

I feel disconnected when…

HOW DID WE BECOME SO DISCONNECTED?

In a world where life moves quickly and you can expect to have almost anything you want when you want it, you may find yourself living in overdrive. When you race from one appointment to the next, eat on the run, drive like a maniac, set unrealistic deadlines, and rush to check off everything on your to-do list, it can be pretty difficult to connect on any level. Overdrive is leaving more people than ever disconnected from relationships. When life feels more like a race than a journey, there is little time to connect in a meaningful way with God, yourself, or anyone else.

Consider your own day-to-day interactions. Are you among the millions of people who are disconnected from the people who live around them? Because people are more mobile today, many individuals and families live hundreds, sometimes thousands of miles from their nearest relatives. Even families who live in the same city are often disconnected by schedules that leave little time for nurturing relationships. Even the friendly next-door neighbor is sadly becoming an anomaly.

When I was growing up, it was considered courteous and quite normal to welcome a new neighbor with a friendly gesture or gift to acknowledge their presence. At the very least, one would expect neighbors to ring the doorbell and introduce themselves. Today people are often too self-absorbed to even wave at, let alone talk to, the people who live around them. And those who are willing to extend neighborly gestures often feel they may be intruding or will be considered nosy if they are too friendly.

Take note of your own attitude toward the people you encounter on a daily basis. Do you ever speak to your neighbors? Do you look the grocery store cashier in the eyes and say hello?

Disconnection is evident not only in our neighborhoods but also in how we communicate. With the invention of the telephone, face-to-face communication was gradually replaced by voice-to-voice communication.

What Your Life Is Saying About Connection

How do you know when you need to make a stronger connection? These are a few of the telltale signs:

- You've learned to live with a job you do not love.
- You feel pressured to live up to other people's expectations.
- Life has become a monotonous routine.
- You feel lost, unsure of your purpose or what direction to take in your life.
- Your relationships with others are filled with turmoil, uneasiness, boredom, or frustration.
- You are angry with God and do not want to work through the issue.
- Making major decisions is a difficult and anxiety-ridden process.
- You do not enjoy spending time alone.
- You do not pray often, or prayer feels like a duty or obligation rather than heartfelt communication with a loving God who wants the best for you.
- You find it difficult to speak up for yourself.
- You feel disconnected from any members of your family.
- Your finances are in disarray.

Now talking on the phone has been replaced to a large extent by e-mail, touch-tone menus, and two-way pagers. We do not have to see people and look at their faces, see their expressions, shake their hands, or experience their humanity. For so many aspects of our personal and business relationships, we simply do not have to talk to people unless we really want to—and if we do want to, it isn't easy.

Technology has given us wonderful conveniences, but in many ways it has impaired our ability to connect in meaningful ways with others. The

The following indicators show that you understand the principle of connection:

- You have a sense of divine purpose and destiny.
- You have a clear and compelling vision that keeps you persevering even in the face of failure and disappointment.
- You seek to learn the life lesson in every experience, even those that are difficult, negative, or tragic.
- You seek and experience spiritual growth on a continual basis.
- You have defined success for yourself.
- Prayer is a part of your daily life and a way of strengthening your spiritual life.
- Your job/business/community involvement is an expression of your innermost values and desires.
- You spend some quiet time alone on a regular basis.
- You communicate openly, honestly, and effectively in your relationships with others.
- Because you fully understand who you are and why you are here, you are confident about making major life decisions.
- Living at your highest potential is a way of life.
- Your financial plans and behavior reflect your vision and values.

late advice columnist Ann Landers once observed, "Television has proved that people will look at anything rather than each other." Media—such as television, movies and the Internet—do more than entertain; in many cases, they replace good, old-fashioned conversation. Some people use television like a drug that numbs them to reality and keeps them from having to spend time with themselves and with those around them. That universal craving for connection leads some people to superficially connect with the people they see and hear on television. They are influenced by the lives, images, and opinions of celebrities. This mode of connection can lead them to adopt ideas and values that do not align with who they truly are.

You and I are bombarded daily with messages that encourage us to spend more time working, less time at home; more time trying to live up to unattainable standards of beauty, less time interacting with each other; more time reaching for shallow standards of success, less time seeking opportunities for contemplation and spiritual reflection. Challenge yourself to dig deeper for the impact of societal messages—both positive and negative—that feed your mind on a daily basis. Is simultaneously working full time and raising a family what you want to do? Or do you feel pressured by societal expectations to be a modern "superwoman"? If that's your path, God will give you the grace to do it, but if it isn't your path, you'll be miserable. Are you constantly comparing yourself with others, analyzing whether your looks, car, house, or wardrobe make it appear that you've stepped out of the pages of *Vogue* or *GQ*? By raising your awareness of these messages, you can more consciously choose which messages to accept and which ones to reject.

As we become aware not only of the wrong messages we receive but also of all the ways in which we've disconnected from God, ourselves, and others, we are freed to begin pursuing those healthy connections once more.

CONNECTING WITH GOD

The Bible says, "Draw near to God and He will draw near to you" (James 4:8). In other words, God is always there, ready for us to talk to Him and seek His direction for our lives—but the first move is ours to make. God's hand is always extended toward you, hoping that you will reach out your hand to His. God will not force His way into your life, but if you take action and reach out to Him, you will begin to experience His divine presence in your life as He draws closer to you and you to Him. As you each take a step toward the other, your hands finally touch His, connecting and releasing divine power into your life. With that power, your potential for success is unlimited.

All you have to do is approach God with a prepared heart and begin to practice spiritual connection on a regular basis, believing that He truly cares about your success.

Connection with God Requires a Pure Heart

In James 4:8, when the writer encourages us to draw near to God, he also tells us to cleanse our hands and purify our hearts. Many people attempt to connect with God selfishly. They know what they want from God but ignore what God wants from them. We can only truly connect with God, however, when our hearts our pure.

Our spiritual lives are in order when we follow the two greatest commandments: "Love the LORD your God with all your heart, with all your soul, and with all your mind," and "Love your neighbor as yourself" (Matthew 22:37,39). In connecting with God on your path to success, it is essential that you listen to your life on a daily basis and ask if your attitude, actions, and thoughts exhibit your love for God and others. That means asking forgiveness when you have done wrong and granting forgiveness to those who have wronged you. It means helping others simply because you can. It means living a life that is pleasing in God's sight and praying for help when that seems too difficult. Having a pure heart means not allowing anything or anyone to hinder your relationship with God.

Many attitudes and behaviors can prevent you from having a pure heart, including:

- pride or ego
- unforgiveness, bitterness, or resentment
- gossip
- wrong motives
- greed or stinginess
- self-centeredness
- envy

Any sin that goes unaddressed in your life will interfere with your ability to connect spiritually. This does not mean that God does not love you or will not hear your prayers. But your progress on your path to success may be hindered until you address every impurity in your life. Proverbs 4:23 says, "Keep your heart with all diligence, for out of it spring the issues of life." What areas in your life do you need to address to ensure that your heart is pure?

God's Interest in Your Success

Purity of heart does not mean that your definition of success will be so spiritual that it excludes a desire for financial wealth or material luxuries. If these are an offspring of your success, then they will flow naturally into your life as you walk down the path you were born to walk. However, rather than being your primary criteria of success, they will be the unique benefits of living at your highest potential.

In the Old Testament, God gave a recipe for success when He instructed Joshua about leading the Israelites following Moses's death:

> This Book of the Law shall not depart from your mouth, but you
> shall meditate in it day and night, that you may observe to do
> according to all that is written in it. For then you will make your
> way prosperous, and then you will have good success. (Joshua 1:8)

God made it clear that in order to find success and prosperity, we must make His Word, the Bible, a priority in our lives. As we meditate on it daily, we grow to know God more intimately, which enables us to connect with Him more easily. Imagine someone proclaiming that he or she wants to get to know you, but at the same time, this person does not express any interest in learning what you value and what is most important to you. Would you believe he or she had a sincere desire to connect with you? Yet this is often how we treat God. He has given us an owner's manual for life, but we must read it and follow it if we are to enjoy "good success."

For many years I did not believe that God was particularly concerned with my success—and certainly not with my desire for financial prosperity. I could not imagine that given everything else God had to be concerned with, He could possibly be interested in my financial plan beyond providing the basics. The more I connect with God, however, the more I realize that He wants to bless me—and He wants to bless you, too. Blessings aren't always financial, of course. Nor would we want them to be.

Psalm 37:4 is one of my favorite scriptures. It says, "Delight yourself…in the LORD, and He shall give you the desires of your heart." We are to enjoy God, communicate with Him, and live our lives as an extension of His love. In other words, when we connect with God, He will plant the seeds of His divine purpose, desires, and aspirations in our hearts—and then bring them into existence.

Getting Plugged In

Connecting with God is like plugging into a power source, such as an electrical outlet. If the battery for your laptop computer is charged because it has been connected to the energy source, the computer will run for a while. But unless it's plugged in again, the battery will eventually run low and the computer will shut down. When you're disconnected from your power source, you can no longer access what you need to operate effectively. In addition, it is highly unlikely that you would be successful if you tried to plug into the outlet while running past it without stopping for a moment. As you haphazardly attempted to shove the prongs into the outlet, you'd probably miss the socket altogether and scratch the wall! Plugging into an electrical outlet is easy, but to do it successfully, you must stop, take your time, and be deliberate about it. The same holds true for expanding and strengthening your relationship with God.

Your daily habits say a lot about what you value and what takes priority in your life. If a hidden camera had recorded your actions over the last week, what would it reveal about your relationship with God? If you truly want to connect with God, then make sure your actions reflect that priority. One way you can do this is to develop three daily spiritual habits— simple but deliberate actions for connecting with God.

I've listed here a number of ways you can incorporate spiritual connection into your daily life. Choose three of these to incorporate into each day—or try out an idea of your own.

Praise and worship. Each day is an opportunity to praise God for the life you've been given. It is also an opportunity to worship with your life.

You do that by allowing your life to be an example of God's love, mercy, forgiveness, and abundance. When you wake up in the morning, ask yourself, How can I serve God today through my actions and my life?

Pray. This is simply a way of communicating your thoughts to God. If you can think, you can pray. Prayer is what you make it. It can be your way of saying thank you, making a request, sharing your thoughts, asking for guidance, or listening for wisdom. Prayer opens the door of spiritual communication.

Meditate. Meditation is a means of quieting your mind and connecting spiritually. It is an extension of prayer. Often during these moments, God communicates to you, giving you wisdom, guidance, and inspiration. But it requires that you stop talking and start listening. Even when you hear nothing, don't be discouraged. Sometimes the answer to your prayer is simply "Be still."

Count your blessings. This is a simple but powerful tool for putting life into perspective. Count at least ten blessings every day—while you are driving or taking a walk or washing dishes. Practice being in a state of continual gratitude.

Keep a spiritual journal. Consider keeping a written record of your prayer requests, answers, inspiring moments, and life challenges. Over time you will be amazed to look back and see the answered prayers and the spiritual growth you have experienced.

Write a letter to God. Sharing your thoughts and prayers with God in the form of a letter can be an intimate way of strengthening your relationship with Him. It doesn't have to be long or elaborate, just honest and sincere. Every now and then when I write to God, He writes back! He fills my spirit with His message for me, and I write it down as quickly as I can.

Read your Bible and spiritually uplifting books. What you feed your mind will ultimately be revealed in your attitudes and actions. Reading

God's Word on a daily basis is a way to build yourself up spiritually through a deeper understanding and knowledge of His plan for successful living.

Enjoy nature. God's amazing goodness is all around us if we will simply take the time to notice it. Appreciate the beauty of nature and the imagination of the Creator by taking a walk, listening to the whistling birds, and enjoying the gentle breeze as it cools your skin on a summer day.

Pay attention to the "sermons in stones." Shakespeare said that there are "sermons in stones."[1] He was right. By tuning in to the lessons all around you, you begin to experience the many avenues of divine communication. God speaks to us through situations, through people, and through His Word. Our job is to tune in so that we can get the lessons He is trying to teach us. You can find yourself in the same situations time and again if you do not learn to view your failures and mistakes as learning tools.

Quiet down enough to hear that still, small voice. Often people embrace noise in an effort to drown out the silence. They turn on the radio, the television, their favorite music CD—anything for a little background noise or a distraction from internal disquiet. But it is in those silent moments that you are able to listen to your life and hear the voice of God directing your steps. You must be willing to clear the clutter that clogs your mind and keeps you from recognizing that still, small voice that can lead you to the path to success. Deliberately spend a day without watching television, listening to the radio, reading the newspaper, or surfing the Internet, and notice how much more connected you feel.

Trust your inner voice. Don't sabotage your own success by failing to trust your inner voice. While you must first quiet down enough to hear the voice, it only becomes valuable to you when you trust the voice enough to

---

1. William Shakespeare, *As You Like It,* act 2, scene 1.

heed it and act on it. It is essential to trust your "sixth sense." It is God's way of communicating to you. By trusting, you take a leap of faith to do things that may not make immediate sense in the physical realm, but spiritually they are right on target.

❦

By connecting with God, who already knows you completely and loves you despite your faults, you gain a new perspective on success—and ultimately, a new perspective on life. Spiritual connection will help you experience firsthand that you are not alone in your journey. God is there to inspire, encourage, comfort, and guide you on a path filled with blessings and opportunities created just for you.

CONNECTING WITH YOURSELF

Many people are not successful because they do not know what they want. And they do not know what they want because they are not in touch—or *connected*—with themselves. Years of living to gain the approval or acceptance of others has confused them into believing that what others want is synonymous with what they want. Most of us have wrestled with this in some area of our lives, but if we make a habit of believing that everyone else is somehow wiser and has the answers, we relinquish the power of our own connection.

Divine messages will at times be delivered through people in your life, but if you are connected with yourself, you will know the difference between heeding someone's advice because it is the right thing for you and heeding it because you don't trust your own inner voice. If you are not honest with yourself about what you want, you end up pursuing dreams, relationships, and material possessions that have no real meaning. Time and time again you will find yourself in situations that are frustrating, unfulfilling, or less than exciting.

On the other hand, you can find the path to fulfilling your true purpose as you connect with yourself by pursuing honesty, asking provocative questions, and practicing self-love.

Get Honest with Yourself

Stephanie said she wanted to transition out of her "secure" corporate management position and begin running her part-time consulting business on a full-time basis. For reasons she could not explain, she felt stuck. One client project was four months behind schedule; she could not seem to get the work done. When I asked Stephanie if she felt stuck in other areas of her life, her fifteen-second pause was followed by a reluctant admission: Her closets were so cluttered she could not see the floor, her laundry consistently piled up until she felt too overwhelmed to start a load in the washer, and her sister, who had asked to stay for two months, had worn out her welcome after nearly nine months.

One by one we addressed issues that on the surface seemed unrelated to her business. Week by week she made progress—first the clutter, then the sister, then a simple system for keeping clothes clean. As she became unstuck in her household, she began uncovering answers about the business. She realized she hated consulting and had no desire to create business plans for other companies. Knowing that her MBA prepared her to do that sort of work, colleagues and friends had suggested she pursue the obvious. They looked to her past to determine what she should do in the future— and she listened.

"What is it that you do that doesn't feel like work when you are doing it?" I asked Stephanie.

"Oh, that's easy," she quickly responded. "I like teaching entrepreneurs how to start and run their businesses successfully. I even have a manual with a methodology I created to help put them on the right path."

Stephanie's story shows that you can have the answers right in front of you, yet allow your fears to blind you to them. Rather than relying on your past or on others for direction, you must be willing to ask yourself the questions that will reveal who you really are and what you really want. Remember, your past may prepare you for your path, but it does not determine your path.

Honesty is essential for connecting with yourself because genuine connection is based on truth. If you lie to yourself or refuse to hear the truth, it is impossible to find your unique path. The truth may not always be pretty, but working through it offers opportunities for growth.

When you find yourself "behaving badly," be willing to ask yourself why. For example, jealousy can often tell you a lot about what you really want. It is unlikely that you will feel jealous of a lifestyle, position, or situation that you don't in some way desire for yourself. Feelings such as jealousy, irritation, anger, and sadness, or issues of control and manipulation can help you discover the real you. So rather than beating yourself up about these negative responses, ask yourself why you feel the way you feel and why you do the things you do. If you are truthful in your answers, you will likely discover a new perspective, idea, or passion.

Ask Yourself Key Questions

One of the best ways to get to know yourself better is to ask and answer questions that identify what you want and why you want it. The "why" gives purpose to your desires. One of the most critical questions is "What values are most important to me?" Values represent who you are and what you are about—and they serve as a compass to direct you to your path. Your values are something you are willing to fight for, and they are aligned with your unique path. People who are extraordinarily successful express their values daily through their relationships, work, finances, spiritual life, and physical activity.

When you are connected spiritually, your values will reflect God's presence in your life. That does not mean, however, that everyone who has a strong relationship with God will have the same core values. Your values are derived from your own passion, talents, and experiences. What are your most important values? Here are a few to consider. Circle only the ones that "grab" you.

excellence	sincerity	truth
adventure	compassion	being a role model
community	ministry	change
freedom	patience	transformation
beauty	control	abundance
humor	courage	spontaneity
accomplishment	risk	victory
empowerment	fun	support
growth	security	energy
creativity	preparation	curiosity
achievement	strategy	communication
education	wealth	love
romance	independence	family
service	charity	expression
partnership	purpose	health
joy	fairness	fitness
sensitivity	righteousness	political consciousness
integrity	holiness	_____
commitment	affection	_____
professionalism	perfection	_____

From the values you circled or wrote in the space provided, identify the three to five that are most important to you:

1.

2.

3.

4.

5.

Always come back to your values as a means of ensuring that the path you are walking is aligned with what is most important to you.

Learn to Love Yourself

Think of one person in this world you love dearly. Close your eyes and imagine yourself with him or her. Think about the things you do together and the ways in which you have been there for each other. If I were to observe your relationship with your loved one, how would I know that you love this person? To answer this question, I would most likely consider your treatment of this individual, your attentiveness, the level of respect you demonstrate, the kinds of things you do for him or her, and your concern for this person's well-being. If you profess your love for someone yet treat that person terribly, I would question your sincerity. For me to believe that you love this individual, your actions need to mirror your profession of love.

It is interesting that most people readily apply this "actions speak louder than words" concept to their relationships with others, but not to their relationship with themselves. Yet loving yourself builds your confidence, self-esteem, and courage to make choices that lead to success. It is not about being self-absorbed and caring only about yourself. It is about acknowledging and meeting your own need to be valued simply for being who you are.

When you are in a loving relationship, your love deepens as it is expressed through your actions toward each other. Over time your acts of love become the foundation of a solid relationship. The same holds true of your relationship with yourself. Each time you stand up for yourself in some way, you are loving yourself. When you take time to treat yourself to a much-needed break, you are loving yourself. When you refuse to beat yourself up for past mistakes, you are loving yourself. When you consciously create a beautiful environment in which to live, you are loving yourself. When you choose to eat healthfully so that your body can function at its optimal level, you are loving yourself.

Consider the following statements in order to gauge whether yours is an attitude of self-love or self-neglect. Place a check mark beside the statements that are true for you:

_____ I put everyone else's desires ahead of my own.

_____ I am uncomfortable saying no when I don't want to do something.

_____ I consider myself too busy to pamper or nourish myself daily.

_____ If I am not feeling well, I am unlikely to rest or take the day off from work.

_____ I put up with rude or inappropriate behavior from others.

_____ I skip meals because of my busy schedule.

_____ I am very hard on myself when I make a mistake, to the point of calling myself names. ("I'm so stupid for doing that" or "How could I be such an idiot?")

_____ I would feel guilty about treating myself to something special, even as a reward for reaching a goal.

If you checked any of these statements, you have some work to do! That's okay, though, because at least you know where you're starting. If most of these statements do not apply to you, you are already in a loving place, and it will be easier for you to make a genuine connection on all levels.

Remember, you want to move from an attitude of self-neglect to the highest level of self-love. In doing so you will experience more peace, joy, and calm, along with less chaos, stress, and aggravation. You will begin to find the "you" that you were meant to be. Nourishing your mind, body, and spirit means you have more of yourself to give to those you love and to what matters most to you. Self-love facilitates the connection with yourself, and it also empowers you to genuinely connect with others.

CONNECTING WITH OTHER PEOPLE

Take a moment to answer these three questions:

1. How did you land the job you have or start the business you own?

2. How did you meet your closest friend?

3. What led you to move to the city where you live, or what compels you to stay there?

A common theme likely runs through your answers to these questions: people. Whether relatives, friends, or even strangers, people connect us with people who help us succeed.

Most people know that intelligence and hard work are two factors that lead to success, but too few of us recognize the importance of relationships to success. Many people are stuck in dead-end jobs not because they don't have the potential to do something more but because they lack the ability to connect with people. If they recognized the importance of being considerate, conscientious, and easy to get along with, opportunity would knock more often and more quickly.

Connection with others enables you to:

- *Fulfill your purpose in life.* Your purpose in life is not simply to use your gifts, but to use your gifts to serve others in a positive way. Your purpose is incomplete if it has no impact on anyone but you.
- *Learn about yourself.* In relationship with other people, you discover your likes and dislikes, your limits and opportunities, what excites and frustrates you. Your interactions with others reveal your character, strengths, and weaknesses.
- *Give and receive love.* A fulfilling life is rich in relationships.
- *Learn and grow without reinventing the wheel.* By studying and learning from the mistakes and failures of others who have gone before you, you can progress along your path much more quickly.
- *Access opportunities that would otherwise be unavailable.* A connected web of relationships allows paths to cross and destinies to be shaped.

As you connect with God and yourself, you will find that opportunities abound to genuinely connect with others. Why is this? In many cases it is because you are living on purpose, walking the path you were meant to walk. God wants to work through you, and that happens most easily when you use your natural gifts, talents, and passion to make a positive impact on the world. When you begin walking your path, opportunities to live your purpose will naturally manifest themselves—and many of these opportunities involve people. As you genuinely connect with people who cross your path, many of them will be a blessing to you, while others will inspire you to be a blessing.

Often we pray for a miracle and wait for it to mysteriously take place. But God frequently uses people to declare His love and demonstrate His miracles. Being aware of the importance of every connection, remaining alert to opportunities to connect, and practicing healthy communication will enable us to be on both the giving and receiving ends of His divine generosity.

The Power of a Single Connection

Take a moment to list your three greatest achievements to date, then note who helped connect you to your dream:

1.

2.

3.

Now ask yourself what connection led you to these people. What connection led you to the people who led you to these people? Go back as far as you can. Amazingly, you may find that many of the key connections you have made trace back to just one or two people or events in your life.

Why is this important? First of all, it illustrates the power of just one connection. If one connection or one event in life can develop into a massive web of opportunities for you, then it is important to recognize the fragility of human connection. Burning a bridge, for example, does not just impact the situation at hand. It can impact opportunities you may never be aware of. A nasty attitude toward just one person could grow into a reputation that drives away people you have never even encountered. Not giving your all for just one performance could mean the difference between connecting or not connecting with the person who happened to cross your path that day—the person who has the means to help you move down your path more quickly.

On the other hand, you can never anticipate all the good that may come from just one connection. Psychologist and legal consultant Phil McGraw thought he was connecting with Oprah Winfrey to defend her against a lawsuit brought on by Texas cattle ranchers. But when his path crossed hers, it changed direction and began to lead him toward an entirely new level of success. If you had told him in 1996 that he would one day host a nationally syndicated television talk show with the highest ratings since the debut of *The Oprah Winfrey Show*, it might have sounded illogical to him.

Look for Opportunities

As you pray and connect with God, ask for wisdom to know when He is connecting you with people for a specific purpose. You may pray for extraordinary success, but if you don't recognize the blessings or opportunities that can catapult you to the next level, you will sabotage your own progress. An important lesson in connecting with others is recognizing that opportunity may present itself at any time. Be prepared to take advantage of the opportunities that cross your path.

What steps can you take to connect better with others?

- Be approachable.
- Be interested in others.
- Seek relationships with people whose values are aligned with yours.
- Listen to what people tell you, and give them your full attention.
- Don't take everything personally.
- Be helpful.
- Don't burn bridges.

- Do your best in every situation. (You never know when God is showcasing your gifts in order to connect you with someone who will help you.)
- See the big picture in every situation.
- Respect others, including their time and resources.
- Smile!
- Connect with God and yourself so that you are clear about who you are.

Practice Healthy Communication

In order to connect with others, you must communicate. Disconnection often occurs when communication channels are clogged with too much unproductive information or too little genuine human interaction. Disconnection also occurs when we do not take the time to genuinely communicate when problems arise.

During a coaching session, my client Dan mentioned an upcoming family gathering that he planned not to attend because of his strained relationship with an older brother. The disconnection in their relationship dated back to elementary school. The older brother had been held back in school and placed in the same grade as Dan, who was a year younger. As Dan excelled academically and socially, his older brother struggled and resented Dan's success. Perhaps they were too young to handle the dynamics of their circumstances, and their parents were oblivious that the praise for Dan's academic success needed to be balanced with praise for his brother's unique talents and accomplishments. For whatever reason, the failure in communication resulted in increased tensions, and what began as a childhood sibling rivalry snowballed into a tangled web of pride, hurt feelings, resentment, and anger. Thirty years later the disconnection was stronger than ever, and Dan was reluctant to attend the gathering for fear that the tension would make the time too uncomfortable.

A top manager in his company as well as a devoted husband and father, Dan yearned for success in his relationship with his brother. "It is frustrating to be successful in so many areas of my life, to have loving relationships with my friends and family, yet not be able to even talk to my own brother," he said in a whisper filled with shame and anxiety.

I asked Dan, "What do you want from your relationship with your brother?"

He replied, "To be able to have a conversation, to act like brothers."

"Why does that matter to you?" I probed.

His answer compelled him to take action: "I don't want to have any regrets if, God forbid, he were to die tomorrow." With that reply he realized he had nothing to lose in reaching out to his brother. Today the relationship is improving, but the communication gap had grown so wide that creating a successful connection between the two will require ongoing patience.

But the struggle will be worthwhile for Dan, no matter the outcome. Why? Because in relationship with other people, you come to know yourself better.

And that's exactly what the principle of connection is all about.

CONNECTION LEADS YOU TO YOUR LIFE PURPOSE

As you connect personally, spiritually, and relationally, you begin to recognize key indicators regarding your unique mission or purpose in life. When you pursue that mission, you walk onto your unique path that leads to extraordinary success.

Within your mission are a multitude of "assignments." For example, if your mission is "to inspire, facilitate, and promote healing to those who are suffering," you might have a wide range of assignments at any given point in time to (1) attend medical school and become a doctor, (2) comfort and encourage a friend or relative who has suffered emotional or physical abuse, (3) be a living example of someone who models a healthy life-style, and (4) share information about healthy living with others as opportunities arise. As you fulfill your various assignments, you will find that, although some of them may be challenging, the help you need to complete your assignments seems to show up—almost effortlessly. And when it doesn't, your life is usually trying to tell you that somewhere you've taken a wrong turn.

When I coach, one of the first things I help clients do is determine their life purpose. We begin by determining their most important values, and then identifying what they are passionate about. Passion is the desire and excitement God places in your heart for a particular cause or activity. Your purpose is the point at which your values meet your passion.

Look back at page 27 as a reminder of what you identified as your top values. Then name five things you are passionate about:

1.

2.

3.

4.

5.

What do you learn by examining your values and the things you are passionate about? What does this information reveal about your purpose in life—the answer to the question, "Why are you here?"

Some people find it challenging to distill their purpose into a few words, so let me give you some examples of the personal missions of people I have coached:

- *Lynn:* "To share love and light through the power of communication." An on-air personality for a smooth-jazz radio station, Lynn has a voice that exudes love and warmth. The love she shares, both personally and professionally, ensures that her mission is not just about work, but about the way she lives her life and impacts those around her.

- *Patricia:* "To inspire beauty and excellence, both inside and out." Patricia is a fashion stylist whose most important values are excellence, beauty, and service. She does everything with style, class, and excellence in a spirit of service to others.
- *Derek:* "To inspire and motivate others, especially in the African American community, to become excellent money managers and effective wealth builders." Derek is growing his financial services business as well as maximizing his family's financial strength so that his finances embody his mission. He is using his MBA degree and his prior work experience, which have led to this point on his path.
- *Michael:* "To do my best at everything I attempt and receive my blessings by helping others reach their goals." Michael says he is blessed with everything he needs, so all that is left is to do his best and be a blessing to other people as they walk their paths to success. When people who cross his path have a goal, he delights in helping them reach it.
- *Kristin:* "To express my creativity through words that inspire thought and emotion in others." A graduate student in film writing, Kristin has already written a novel and a screenplay. Through her attitude and the way she lives, she expresses creativity daily.

Did you know that Jesus had a mission statement too?

- *Jesus:* "I have come that they may have life, and that they may have it more abundantly" (John 10:10). Everything Jesus did during His three years of ministry served this purpose. Whether He was healing the sick, giving sight to the blind, teaching and preaching, or giving His life to save the world—all served to help fulfill His greater purpose.

THE NEXT STEP

When you connect on all three levels—with God, self, and others—you can begin to identify the direction your life should take. But you also need to examine your fears, questions, and challenges if you're to overcome them and move toward success. In the next chapter we'll examine the principle of self-curiosity, which will prepare you to do just that.

❧ WALKING YOUR PATH ❧

Listen to Your Life: How Well Connected Are You?

Place a check mark in front of every statement that is true for you.

_____ I feel certain about my decisions at least 90 percent of the time.

_____ I pray daily. I rarely go even one day without prayer.

_____ I find it very easy to answer questions such as "What brings you joy?" and "What do you love to do?"

_____ I know my top five values.

_____ I know my purpose in life.

_____ I relate easily to a wide variety of people.

_____ I personally know people who can help me reach my goals.

_____ I feel comfortable asking for help from people who are able to help me.

_____ I can easily say no to people when I need to.

_____ I consistently listen to my life and take action based upon what I hear.

_____ I trust myself to handle relationships, money, and all aspects of my life in the best way.

_____ I trust God to direct my path when I am unclear about what direction to take.

_____ I love myself exactly the way I am today.

If you were able to check all of these statements, congratulations! You are well connected. Stay on your path. If you were unable to check all of the statements, make it a priority to begin connecting on a deeper level.

5-Minute Action Step

Carve out five minutes today and identify the three daily spiritual habits you would like to practice. Add them to your appointment calendar for the coming month.

1.

2.

3.

48-Hour Challenge

Using connection as your foundation, during the next two days, identify the path that is calling you. Answer these essential questions:

1. Am I on my divinely ordained path? If so, what is the purpose of my path?

2. If I am not currently on my path, in what direction do I sense God leading me? What steps will I need to take to get there?

❧ PRAYER OF CONNECTION ❧

Enable me to connect easily with You, with myself, and with others. Sometimes the challenges of life shout so loudly that I cannot hear myself think, let alone hear Your still, small voice. I want to hear from You. Help me not only to hear but to listen and take action based upon what You reveal to my spirit. Ignite within me the power to connect continually with You and with myself. Grant me the confidence to fully be myself. Give me the courage to say no to experiences that do not allow me to wholly express who I am as well as Your presence in my life. Show me how to say what I mean and mean what I say when communicating with others. Allow me to encounter people on my path whom I can bless and who can be a blessing to me. Strengthen my relationships so that they will enhance my purpose in life rather than distract me from it. "Show me Your ways, O LORD; teach me Your paths." Psalm 25:4 *Give me the strength, wisdom, desire, and courage to do Your will. I pray that I will always listen to my life so that I can reconnect where I am disconnected and walk onto the path I was born to walk. Amen.*

SELF-CURIOSITY

Exploring Who You Are and What You Want

And you shall know the truth,
and the truth shall make you free.

—JOHN 8:32

D uring a deep conversation with a wise and curious woman several years ago, she posed an intriguing question: "Do you think the people in your life should love you for being?"

My dumbfounded response later haunted me. "For being *what?*" I frowned. I didn't understand the question, and for some reason, I didn't like it either. *People don't love you for being,* I thought to myself. *What good are you just being if you're not doing something?* At that point in my twenty-four-year-old mind, what made me lovable was not who I was, but what I was and what I had accomplished. Her question lingered like the bitter aftertaste of thick, nasty medicine. I didn't like it, but it was the catalyst for healing my misconceptions.

As I delved into my response, I realized that I held no one else to the standard I had set for myself. I knew that my family and friends did not love me for what I did, but for who I was, yet I continued to perform as though I were earning their love. Although family and friends who knew me were unaffected by my unhealthy attitude, I attracted relationships that fed into my subconscious pattern of achievement-based love. Then I would find myself unhappy and frustrated for attracting people who were more enamored with image and achievements than with substance and character.

During this time more questions began to plague me: If I want to be loved for being, then who am I? How can I be more of who I am? How can I be true to myself? If I am true to myself, will that make my life more meaningful? Who have I been sent into this world to be?

I began to answer my questions, bewildered by some of them but deeply enlightened by my responses.

SELF-CURIOSITY LEADS TO SELF-TRANSFORMATION

The best answers always come when we pose questions that get to the core of an issue. The questioning of oneself for the purpose of personal and spiritual growth is what I call "self-curiosity." This principle provides you with the tools you need to address the fears, distractions, and challenges that threaten to divert you from extraordinary success.

Self-curiosity challenges your beliefs and bad habits, helps you identify the annoyances that drain your energy, and gives you the insight to recognize and avoid the distractions that can lure you onto a less-than-fulfilling path. If connection places you squarely onto your path, self-curiosity minimizes the potential obstacles on that path. Some difficulties, of course, will be beyond your control—a layoff, illness, the loss of a loved one, or a downturn in the economy. Many challenges, however, are within your control and can be overcome through changing your environment, your thinking, or your approach. But before you can resolve such issues, you have to employ self-curiosity to get to the root of the problem.

Through self-curiosity, you learn from mistakes and envy, happiness and disappointment. Over time, challenges that once seemed insurmountable will become stepping stones to success. Rather than running from issues, you face them with courage and say, "You know what? You've been here too long. I'm tired of your stealing my joy and my moments. It's time for you to go." We grow by questioning our actions, noticing our intentions, and seeking our healthiest mental, spiritual, and emotional state of being.

One of the greatest spiritual truths is that we are not human beings having a spiritual experience; rather, we are spiritual beings having a human experience. Consider that for a moment. You are not your body, your color, your role, your nationality, your title. You are your spirit. Think about it. Your spirit is the only part of you that has been the same your entire life. Your face may change, your voice may change, your social status may change, and your body may change, but your spirit is the same as it was when you were a child. You are the same person—perhaps wiser and better, but still *you*. If you lack the courage to transform, the fears and quirks that controlled you yesterday will continue to control you your entire life. Transformation occurs when you choose to practice a healthy habit of self-curiosity.

Sometimes, self-curiosity can provoke heated emotions. You may be unenthusiastic about exploring certain questions. *Can we do this another day?* your spirit begs. *That hurts too much.* If you proceed gently and honestly, though, the pain will give birth to purpose and momentum. At other times your answers will fill you with excitement and joy. *Yes!* your spirit sings in celebration of a light-bulb moment or a breakthrough. *She finally got it!*

Self-curiosity can be likened to the birth of a child. The delivery process is agonizing, but the end result is life-changing.

Asking the Right Questions

Following are three types of self-curiosity questions:

1. *Expansive questions.* These questions are designed to expand your thoughts beyond your current experiences. They invite you to take a peek at a bigger dream. They challenge you to

---

What Your Life Is Saying About Self-Curiosity

Here are some of the symptoms of failing to practice self-curiosity:

- You have allowed fear or distractions to keep you from walking onto your divinely ordained path.
- The same challenges plague you repeatedly. (For example, you lose weight, gain it back, lose weight, and gain it back again in a vicious, repetitive cycle.)
- You are not taking action to address or overcome the fear that is keeping you stuck.
- You have not identified the beliefs that are holding you back.
- You know what beliefs are holding you back but have not identified or embraced new beliefs based in truth.
- You ignore bad habits that are sabotaging your success, such as overeating, overspending, smoking, laziness, poor time management, bad temper, or procrastination.
- You make excuses—"I don't have enough time, money, education, space, skills, or *whatever*"—instead of taking action.

---

see the big picture. For example, "How would it feel to earn three times as much money?" or "In what ways would you have to change in order to have the kind of marriage that others aspire to?"

2. *Probing questions.* These "why" questions help you understand the reasons for your actions and reactions along your path. For example, "Why did you react that way to this particular situation?" "Why do you want what you want?" or "Why are you afraid?" The purpose of a probing question is to explore your feelings and provide information that will empower you to

- When an obstacle appears on your path, you see it as a stop sign.
- You are not growing, or your path is not expanding to include more fulfillment in the five key life areas: your spiritual life, your physical health and environments, your relationships, your work, and your finances and resources.

What happens when self-curiosity is incorporated into your daily routine?
- You stop obsessing about your problems and start solving them.
- You are compelled to be truthful with yourself because you understand that truth is the basis for real and lasting change.
- You move along your path at a faster pace.
- You consistently make time for self-reflection, often during workouts and while driving.
- You tell yourself the truth, even when the truth about your thoughts or behavior is unflattering or painful.
- You are vigilant about clearing your path of self-imposed or self-sabotaging challenges.
- As you learn and grow, you raise your standards to a higher level.

change your thoughts and ultimately your actions. In self-curiosity, the key is not to judge your feelings, but to use them to gather information about yourself.

3. *Action questions.* These questions challenge you to move forward in some way. "What are you going to do about it?" "What is the next step?" and "When is the deadline?" If your discoveries don't result in action, there's no point in asking the questions.

Just a few pages from here, we'll launch out together on a journey of self-curiosity with questions that provoke thought, fear, excitement, and anticipation of your possibilities. As your spirit steers you on your path, more questions—ones that only you could know to ask—will come to you. Write them down. Answer them. Embrace self-curiosity with curiosity. Open your mind to transformation.

Listening to Your Emotions

Many of us are afraid of our emotions; we've been taught to hide and ignore them. Others of us allow our emotions to rule our lives, controlling our decisions and even destroying our relationships.

When you adopt a healthy attitude toward your emotions, you won't ignore them, nor will you allow them to control you; instead, you'll try to learn from them. Self-curiosity enables you to listen to your emotions and discern what they are trying to tell you. Negative emotions are often indicators that something has changed or needs to change. For example, frustration tells you that something is not working and you need to make a change. But rather than focusing on the frustration, you can ask yourself questions that will help uncover a solution to eliminate your frustration.

Whether you decide to take action or to sit still, listening to your emotions can help you delve more quickly into the truth, and it will ultimately steer you toward your path. What negative emotions are you feeling in the five key areas of your life? As a starting point in your self-exploration, consider the following emotions:

anger	loss
guilt	fear
frustration	anxiety
disappointment	embarrassment
unworthiness	uneasiness
loneliness	overload
regret	feeling overwhelmed
hurt	

Choosing the Right Answers

As you focus on your personal and spiritual growth, you may feel pressured to come up with the "right" answers to your questions. You may also be tempted to give surface answers to the questions. Remember, your questions are for your spirit, that deepest, truest part of yourself. Only through pure, honest exploration can you experience spiritual and personal lightbulb moments—when your spirit emerges with an answer that sheds love and light where there was once darkness, confusion, or bewilderment.

Pure exploration simply means that you engage in self-curiosity for the love of yourself and a desire to explore who you are and what you want and need most so that you can walk confidently, joyfully, and boldly onto your unique path. Through prayer and divine connection, God will point you in the direction to explore. Be curious about your feelings, actions, and experiences. Rather than focusing on any negative issues you might discover about yourself, focus on the growth you will experience when you get to a point of moving forward with your life in the best possible way.

As you begin to answer life's questions with honesty and curiosity, you will begin to appreciate your own humanity. "This is what life is about," you realize. "Learning and growing spiritually, becoming better than I am, and serving the world with purpose. All of this requires growth." You will begin to see how everything in your life fits together perfectly—both the good and the bad. You will begin to notice patterns, healthy ones as well as problematic ones. This process of appreciating your own humanity makes decisions easier and less intimidating, and you will realize that it is okay to explore your thoughts and feelings without any expectation of commitment.

If, for example, you are considering a move to another city to find opportunities that better support your mission, explore the idea and your feelings about moving, recognizing that pure exploration is just that, exploration. It is spiritual fact finding that may lead you to try something new or lead you to stay put. If you consistently get unsatisfactory results in relationships or career endeavors, a spiritual dialogue in the form of self-curiosity can help you discover new ways to proceed. It all begins with asking the right questions and answering them honestly: Why does the same thing keep happening to me? What is not working for me? What could I do differently? What *will* I do differently, and when?

Making Self-Curiosity a Habit

How can you effectively engage in self-curiosity and make it a regular part of your life?

- Begin by answering the questions in the five key areas of fulfillment that follow later in this chapter.
- Develop your own questions as you notice themes and patterns in your thoughts, actions, and feelings.
- At the start of your day, ponder one self-curiosity question while you exercise or stretch.
- Keep a journal of your answers to the questions in this chapter, and develop an action plan based on your responses.

The Writing Habit

One of the best ways to engage in self-curiosity is to write on a daily basis. When many people think of writing, they think of grammar and sentence structure or of being forced to churn out a report. But the type of writing I'm suggesting is not intended for anyone but you. It's a creative opportunity to learn about yourself and grow.

Recording your answers to the questions on the following pages will help you begin to incorporate writing into your daily life. You can take a pragmatic approach and use a simple notebook. Or, if you prefer, you can select a journal that expresses something about you—pretty or oversized, businesslike or spiritually uplifting. Choose something that feels good to you.

Like a wise friend, my writing often speaks to me. You'll find the same thing when you begin writing consistently. I suggest carving out time just after you awaken, work out, or engage in your three daily spiritual habits. You can ask questions. Make observations. Complain. Celebrate. Plan. Hope. Dream. Envision. Share your confusion, frustrations, and disappointments.

When you are in constant connection with God through your three daily spiritual habits, you will find that writing can become a means of communicating with and hearing from God.

Just Do It

The questions that follow will help you begin to explore the five key areas of your life:

- your spiritual life
- your physical health and environments
- your relationships (family, love, friendships, and community)
- your work
- your finances and resources

There is no wrong or right way to answer these questions. The important step is to simply begin, answering the questions at your own pace. Do not try answering all of them now. Answer the one question that stands out on the page, that tugs at your emotions—this is the question your spirit wants to address first. Feel free to bounce from one essential area of life to another.

Be aware that you will resist answering some questions. Move forward with courage and explore them anyway. If a question makes you feel defensive or seems intrusive, explore those feelings further. Deliberately choose not to judge yourself, knowing that you feel what you feel regardless of whether you want to feel that way. Once you acknowledge your response, you can work to adjust your feelings and your thoughts so that they align with your path.

Also note that if you begin to feel defensive about a particular question, you are probably on the trail of something important. It's time to delve deeper. Question your emotions. Ask yourself, What am I afraid of? Dig out the issues. Explore. Pray for guidance, wisdom, and the ability to understand yourself. God is with you, and He is directing your path. Proverbs 3:5-6 says, "Trust in the LORD with all your heart, and lean not on your own understanding; in all your ways acknowledge Him, and He shall direct your paths."

SELF-CURIOSITY QUESTIONS

Spiritual Life

1. In what ways am I fulfilling my life purpose? What more do I want to do to fulfill my calling during my lifetime?

2. What have I been most angry or frustrated with God about? When, and why?

3. For what ten blessings in my life am I most grateful?

4. If I could have a face-to-face conversation with God right now, what three questions would I most like Him to answer? Have I asked those questions in prayer?

5. In what situations have I been responding with anger, frustration, or lack of forgiveness? How could I replace my negative attitudes with love?

6. What three desires would I most like God to fulfill in my life? How can I exercise patience, gratefulness, and cooperation as God responds to these desires?

7. In what areas of my life do I struggle most? How could my relationship with God help me win the struggle over this issue? *Note:* The areas in which we struggle vary widely because of our individual personalities and situations, but here are a few areas to consider as you ponder your answer to this question:

forgiveness	gambling	self-care
bitterness	laziness	worry
pride	hatred	fear
envy	acceptance	arrogance
lying	judgmental attitude	trust
doubt	temper	anger
confidence	emotional stability	promiscuity
sexuality	patience	time management
overspending	self-control	control issues
overeating	self-esteem	

Physical Health and Environments

1. In what area(s) do I need to take better care of myself physically? What action(s) am I willing to take?

2. How do I feel when I decide to put myself first? Guilty? Empowered? Selfish? Why?

3. When was my last complete physical, and when will I schedule my next one?

4. When do I find myself indulging in unhealthy habits? Why?

5. What habits are having a negative impact on my health or physical well-being? What am I willing to do to make a change?

6. How do I feel when I am alone in complete peace and quiet? Am I comfortable or uncomfortable? Do I get bored easily, feel the urge to make a phone call, or turn on the television or some other background noise?

7. What bothers me most about my environments? What am I willing to do this week to create a sanctuary from stress at work? in my car? at home?

Relationships

As you consider the following questions, note that the people in your life can fit into more than one category:

- immediate family (parents, children, spouse, siblings)
- family (includes everyone you are related to)

- loved ones (which may include friends whom you love or who are like family)
- friends
- acquaintances
- colleagues and coworkers
- clients and customers
- fellow citizens

1. With whom would I most like to build a relationship during the coming year? In what ways might this relationship differ from my existing relationships, and how would this relationship enhance or enrich my life?

2. *If you are married:* What makes my spouse feel loved? What makes me feel loved?

If you are single: What are the ten most important qualities I desire in my ideal mate? Do I exemplify the same qualities I seek?

3. Who are the three most important people in my life? Is there a conflict or problem that needs to be resolved in any of these relationships? If so, what first step could I take to resolve it?

4. What relationships are draining my energy? What am I willing to do about it? When?

5. What payoff am I receiving for remaining in a relationship that isn't working?

6. What am I afraid that people will find about me? Why?

7. Who in my life loves me simply for being who I am? Who in my life is more impressed with what I do, who I know, or my accomplishments? How do I feel about it?

Work

Your work is an extension of you. Whether you are paid or unpaid, a CEO, a mail-room clerk, or a stay-at-home caregiver or parent, your life's work provides an opportunity for you to express the values most dear to you. Listen closely to your life as you answer these questions:

1. How does my current primary work allow me to express my natural gifts and talents?

2. What does my ideal work life look like?

3. What are the top five indicators that show I am successful in my work?

4. Who is my mentor, and how can I best use the insights, opportunities, and wisdom he or she has to offer? In return, how can I best express my appreciation for this person?

5. If I lost my job tomorrow, what options would I most want to explore? Is it time to start exploring those options now?

6. In what ways does my work impact my relationships, finances, and spiritual growth?

7. Ten years from now, what will I wish I had done during this period of my career?

Finances and Resources

Your true wealth is measured by more than how much money you have in the bank. Here are some additional resources to consider as you answer the following questions. Feel free to include additional ones as you consider the resources with which you have been blessed.

- time
- talent
- money
- financial access or support
- powerful connections
- family support
- creativity
- specific skills
- _____
- _____
- _____

1. Of the resources available to me, which three—in priority order—are most abundant in my life?

2. What resources or opportunities are going unused or are being underused in my life? What can I do to better utilize them?

3. How do my resources help me take steps on the path to the life that I was born to live?

4. What resource do I want more of, and what actions could I take to acquire more of this resource?

5. How have I wasted resources in the past? What is the greatest lesson I learned as a result?

6. In what ways can I dramatically improve my existing talents? If I made these improvements, what impact would it have on my life?

7. What improvements are needed in my personal finances as they relate to the following areas:
   • financial education
   • debt
   • savings
   • credit report
   • investments
   • taxes
   • real estate
   • business
   • giving

Keep Going

I hope you felt something stir within as you answered the questions in this chapter. Perhaps they provoked thought, fear, excitement, and anticipation of your possibilities.

The questions in this chapter can serve as a self-coaching tool, so refer to them whenever you feel stuck. As you follow your path, more questions—ones that only you could know to ask—will come to you. Write them down and answer them. Use the power of connection to allow the truth of your answers to stimulate your curiosity about how and when to move forward.

The information you gather through self-curiosity can help you to not only determine which areas of your life most need your attention right now but also create an action plan for meaningful change. As you continue to employ this method of listening to your life, your personal and spiritual growth will stay at the forefront of your mind. You'll learn to challenge yourself to stretch beyond your comfort zone and live more fully day by day.

The principle of vision discussed in the next chapter will help give focus to your connections and self-curiosity as you begin to see clearly how everything in your life is designed to lead you toward extraordinary success.

Are you listening?

❧ Walking Your Path ❧

Listen to Your Life: You Have the Answers

Place a check mark in front of every statement that is true for you.

____ I am making measurable progress in the five key areas of my life: spiritual life, physical health and environments, relationships, work, finances and resources.

____ I am comfortable questioning my behavior, thoughts, and feelings.

____ I am willing to listen for the messages my emotions are sending me.

____ I am open to answering the hard questions because I am ready to overcome problems, attitudes, and obstacles that have previously held me back.

____ Even if I cannot answer a question "right," I am willing to ponder the question.

____ I am excited by questions that cause me to think of my life in a way I have not considered.

If you checked off all of the above statements, you have openly embraced the concept of self-curiosity as a means of accelerating your personal growth and overcoming obstacles on your path. If you checked only a few of the above statements, it is even more important to embark on a path of self-curiosity. If you would like support in the process, enlist the help of a coach. If the process is emotionally overwhelming, consider talking with a counselor or psychologist about the issues that bring up the most emotional tension for you. Before you can create the future you want, it is imperative to resolve the past. Ask God to show you how. Then trust His ability to heal the wounds of your past, help you forgive and let go of grudges, and free you from attitudes and beliefs that are holding you back.

5-Minute Action Step

Carve out five minutes today to answer the question that stands out most to you in this chapter. Explore your thoughts on the topic and use your imagination to describe how the best outcome could be manifested in your life.

48-Hour Challenge

In the next forty-eight hours, listen to your life. What is causing you pain, frustration, or continual challenges? Why do you think the problem has shown up in your path? Problems not only teach us lessons, but they have the potential to open the door to opportunities. The key is to stop *having* problems and start *solving* them. Rather than focusing exclusively on the problem, ask yourself questions that lead to a solution. Then take the first step toward implementing it.

✒ PRAYER OF SELF-CURIOSITY ✒

I ask You for the wisdom to better understand myself and to ask myself questions that lead me in the right direction. Your Word says, "If any of you lacks wisdom, let him ask of God, who gives to all liberally and without reproach, and it will be given to him. But let him ask in faith, with no doubting, for he who doubts is like a wave of the sea driven and tossed by the wind." James 1:5-6 *I have no doubt, God, that You will give me the wisdom I need to deal with the issues I face as well as the emotions that come with them. Remove all fear of facing the truth about my feelings. I know that truth is a sign of Your presence and that You take no part in deceit. Help me to hear You clearly so that I am not distracted by lies and confusion. Help me listen to my life so that I can practice self-curiosity as a way of living. When I ask the right questions but cannot seem to uncover the answers, help me connect more deeply with You and with myself so that I can deepen my understanding of my own behavior. Lastly, Lord, steer me away from dwelling on my past and help me focus on restoring and maintaining mental and spiritual health in every area of my life. Amen.*

VISION

Creating a Clear and Compelling Picture of Your Ideal Life

If you can see the invisible, you can do the impossible.
—BISHOP T. D. JAKES

Connection places you on your unique path, and self-curiosity enables you to minimize the obstacles along the way, but the principle that empowers you to stay the course is vision. A vision that vividly illustrates your destination will drive you, motivate you, and give power to the steps you take. A compelling vision is conceived with purpose and clothed with passion. It is specific. It is powerful. It excites.

Those who create a great vision are those who see what others cannot.

One of the greatest visionaries in American history, Reverend Dr. Martin Luther King Jr. shared a vision from the steps of the Lincoln Memorial on August 28, 1963. He painted a picture of a future point on the nation's path, a point that seemed impossible to many of the millions watching by television and to the 200,000 people gathered before him. The picture he painted decades ago still serves as a standard by which the progress of racial harmony in America can be measured. Reverend King passionately illustrated the injustices and glaring inequality that plagued that time period, yet he helped all Americans see that his dream for the future was not just a "black" dream but "a dream deeply rooted in the American dream." He painted a picture that challenged America to live up to its full potential, the premise upon which this country was built: "We hold these truths to be self-evident: that all men are created equal...." He summed up the desire of millions when he described in his vision a hope that his children would "one day live in a nation where they will not be judged by the color of their skin but by the content of their character."

The vision Reverend King projected to the country that day was so specific and so vivid that even today we can read his words and measure just how close we are to fulfilling it.

Reverend King was clearly on a unique and divinely ordained path— a path with a purpose fueled by a powerful vision. His vision, along with his actions, was the catalyst that galvanized millions of people to push America toward fulfilling the potential declared by its founders. As you read his words, and if you have ever listened to the speech in its entirety, you see an illustration that is so vivid, so passionate, and so full of truth.

Your own vision may not spark the revolution of a nation, but it can still evoke passion, truth, and a vivid illustration of the direction your life can take. Your vision will create an overall picture of your ideal life, and as you consider your goals for various aspects of your life, you will find it effective to also create visions that support the grand vision. It is like a family tree with the "grand vision" as the trunk and "subvisions" branching off from it. These subvisions include a vision for your family, marriage or singleness, your finances, health and well-being, your spiritual life, your career, your relationships, and even projects that are important to you.

ENVISIONING YOUR BEST FUTURE

Early one morning as I was writing God a letter in my spiritual journal, the vision for this book came to me like an unexpected gift landing at the doorstep of my mind. What I saw first was the title. It struck a chord because I know the deep satisfaction of following my inner voice. I envisioned the harmony that could exist in our world if all of us listened to our lives and served one another with the natural gifts and talents that allow us to live at the highest level of success.

That vision compelled me to bring this book to life. I envisioned your reading it and being deeply fulfilled as you move onto your path and into your destiny. As I speak, answer e-mails, and coach individuals with diverse backgrounds, issues, and interests, I notice that those who struggle most have strayed far from their own unique path. In fact, they are so out of touch with their spirit, they are blinded to the possibilities for change, unable to catch a glimpse of the life they were born to live. In my vision, I saw you peeling away the layers of mistaken priorities and outside pressures so that you could finally *see* what your life is dying to offer you.

Your God-given path offers abundant blessings and opportunities, but if you've strayed from that path—forcing things to happen and struggling in your relationships, work, or finances—you'll never see them. In my vision you dare to imagine bliss, greatness, purpose, and life prosperity. Because my purpose in life is inspiring people to live more fulfilling lives, my vision for *Listen to Your Life* resonated with my spirit and compelled me to begin writing.

That's what a vision does. It allows you to see yourself where you have never been and believe that you will get there.

When Marilyn came to me for coaching, she said she was "pretty happy" with her job and life but was ready to more fully live out her values and her life purpose on a daily basis. We identified her purpose as motivating young people to excel. One of her key values is freedom, and although she had some freedom with her schedule as a college professor, she felt limited in how much time she could devote to her purpose. She did her best to motivate the students in her courses, but it wasn't enough. And while she liked the flexibility of not having a nine-to-five position, her schedule from week to week was set in stone. What once seemed like freedom had come to feel like a trap. At one time, teaching was her dream, but now she felt called in a new direction. It was time for a new vision.

"What would your ideal work life look like?" I asked her.

After running through a diverse list of possibilities, she said in an excited tone, "I would love to have a schedule I control, so I can coach and speak on topics that help people improve their lives. I am tired of dealing with the politics of my work environment; it's draining me. I want to be free to talk about the topics I am most passionate about."

When I asked Marilyn to create a vision for a career change, she produced one that challenged her and required her to step out in faith. Yet she fully believed she could accomplish this vision.

By connecting with God and herself, she heard the restlessness in her spirit. She realized that it was more than just discontentment; it was a sign that she needed to make a change. Most important, she believed firmly enough in her vision to hire a coach, get training, learn new business skills, and go for it! Consistently taking one action at a time, she stepped into the vision she had created for herself.

A Compelling Vision Is Vivid

To make your vision clear and compelling, you must be specific. When you paint a detailed vision in your mind of where you are headed, the vision compels you to keep moving forward. With a vivid vision you dare to dream of things that may be hard to imagine right now. It allows you to feel, taste, smell, hear, and see the possibilities.

Rather than saying you want to be an entrepreneur, get married, have a family, and make a good living, paint a detailed picture of your ideal life. Describe in full detail what kind of business you want, whom you will serve, what you will offer, what your mission will be, where you will be located, what kind of people will work with you. Describe your ideal spouse— including values, characteristics, attitudes, spiritual beliefs, background— and your ideal relationship. Then describe what kind of family you want, when you want it, where you will live, how many children you want—your own or adopted—how you want to raise them, and whether one of you will stay home. Next, define "good living" and describe what you feel you must have, how you plan to achieve your financial goals, what your risk tolerance is, when you want to retire, how much debt and savings you are comfortable with, what material things you consider essential, and so on.

Be specific about what you want in every aspect of your vision. Specificity ignites excitement, while vagueness results in disinterest. When you can paint a clear mental picture, your mind will move you to action to carry out the plans for your vision.

Perhaps you have said to yourself, Someday I am going to have my own business. When you have a vivid vision, it sounds more like this: Two years from now, I am leaving my current position to make the leap into entrepreneurship. I am beginning to lay the groundwork today by lowering my expenses, eliminating my debt, talking with investors, and building a financial cushion that will allow me to live for at least one full year without a paycheck. My marketing strategy and consulting services will be targeted to medium-size companies in the five- to fifty-million-dollar range, much like the company I work for now. I will have Fridays off and will triple my current income. I will work from home and serve only clients whom I am enthusiastic about.

The more vivid your vision, the more courageous you become about moving forward. Suddenly you believe in it!

A Compelling Vision Requires Faith

We've all heard the skeptical adage "I'll believe it when I see it." When it comes to creating a powerful vision for your life, adopting the I'll-believe-it-when-I-see-it attitude makes it unlikely that you will ever see "it" at all. Why? Because this attitude is lacking in faith. You must first believe your vision is possible, knowing that with God all things are possible.

On your unique path, faith enables you to step forward, confident in the destination of your vision even if the route is unclear. In fact, those with blind faith—those who use the power of divine guidance even when they cannot see how things will work out—tend to find the most success.

Keeping your vision at the forefront of your mind will help you move forward even when your efforts don't appear to be bringing results. Imagine that each blessing and opportunity is like the fruit of sweet-smelling trees along a wooded path. This fruit gives you energy and motivation to move forward. When you begin on your path, you may find just enough fruit to sustain you with the energy you need to keep walking. At times you don't see any fruit at all, but you keep walking toward the sweet and fragrant aroma that indicates heavy-laden trees just ahead.

That fragrance is like the sense of inner knowing that resonates in your spirit when you connect on all levels to discover your divine path. Even without clear evidence, you *know* you are on the right path by the sweet aroma of your gifts, talents, desires, and destiny. Hebrews 11:1 defines *faith* as "the substance of things hoped for, the evidence of things not *seen*" (emphasis added). The blessings and opportunities you anticipate on your path are "the things hoped for." The guidance you receive through your connection with God, yourself, and others is your "evidence of things not seen."

What Your Life Is Saying About Vision

How do you know when you need to create a new vision or upgrade an old one?

- Your vision for your life doesn't enter your thoughts on a daily basis.
- Your vision does not inspire or excite you.
- You have achieved the vision you previously created and need a bigger vision that will stretch you beyond where you are now.
- Your vision can be accomplished without any great leap of faith.
- You created your vision without asking for God's input.
- You created your vision based on someone else's opinion of what you should do.
- Your life lacks a sense of direction even if you feel connected.

How do you know that your vision can propel you toward extraordinary success?

- You are naturally motivated to bring your vision to fruition.
- You believe in your vision with all of your heart, mind, and spirit.
- Your vision is intrinsically connected with your purpose.
- Your vision is written down and straightforward. (Habakkuk 2:2 says, "Write the vision and make it plain on tablets.")
- As you connect with God, you feel a sense of peace about your vision.
- The vision is so compelling to you that nothing will lure you away from it.

CREATING YOUR VISION

Your ability to create a compelling vision depends upon your employing the principles of connection and self-curiosity. Listening to God, yourself, and others and asking questions that help you work through challenges will help you gain a healthy perspective and will ensure that your perception is accurate.

Listen to Nudges of the Spirit

On a sunny Saturday afternoon in July 1999, an unexpected connection gave me the purpose that led to my building a personal vision. For more than two years, I had prayed to know my purpose with certainty and clarity. While browsing in a Seattle bookstore, I felt the sudden and warm embrace of God's presence as I had never felt it before. As it engulfed me, I heard a clear and simple message—not with my ears but in my spirit: "Your mission is to help people live fulfilling lives, and you'll do it through writing and speaking."

I was ecstatic! *That's it!* I thought. *That's really it!* No vision accompanied this revelation of my life purpose. God gave me the mission; it was up to me to "hope for" something to fulfill it, to discover the "assignments" that would help me live it out daily.

Inklings buried in the back of my "someday" file years earlier had given me a glimpse of the vision I was to create. Once I uncovered my mission and set out to create a vision to fulfill it, I drew on the "inklings" and "nudges" that related to my mission. Inklings and nudges are thoughts and ideas that resonate with you, divine messages delivered through the Holy Spirit. The more quickly you listen to them, the easier it will be to move in the right direction. You may not be able to act on them immediately, but you definitely want to keep them safely tucked away in your mind.

Better yet, write them down. A journal of these messages will help you connect the pieces of your vision as they are revealed over time.

My first inkling came in 1991 while in college in Monterey, California. I happened to see motivational speaker Les Brown on public television. I was absolutely taken with the content and excitement of his empowering and entertaining message. I remember thinking, *I want to do that one day. I believe I can.* I tucked that thought away. *Once I've found success in business and life, I'll use my experiences and the wisdom gained to inspire people.* Until my epiphany eight years later, I had not given this inkling much thought.

The second inkling came to me during graduate school. As I pulled up to my apartment one day after class, out of the clear blue sky, this thought came to mind: *I want to write books. That's my dream. I want to do work that has a positive impact on people and gives me the freedom to work at my own pace.* That thought was tucked way in 1994, but its role in my vision became clear after my epiphany in the bookstore.

For some people, the epiphany about inspiring others through writing and speaking might not have sparked a vision for writing books. They might have been compelled to write magazine articles, poetry, screenplays, or novels. Their vision for speaking might have been to work one-on-one with people as a therapist or counselor. Many options exist for your vision, but whatever shape it takes, it should excite you and fuel a passion in you.

What inklings have you had about the direction of your life path? What ideas have been prompted in your spirit? What spiritual nudges have been tucked away in the depths of your imagination?

Be Open to Ideas from Others
Your vision will be multifaceted, so keep your eyes and ears open to ideas you may never have considered. Often you find these ideas as you talk with

others. Their experiences—and their ability to provide an outside perspective on your life—often present rich opportunities for the expansion or adjustment of your vision. As you grow through self-curiosity, you will also be open to new ideas and ways of considering your vision.

After I sold my public relations agency in early 2001, people repeatedly suggested that I do something in broadcasting, particularly television. At first I accepted their comments as compliments. But after about the thirtieth time, it occurred to me that I should take this as more than flattery and incorporate it into my vision. Perhaps God was sending me a message.

So I used the power of connection to communicate my desires to the

Building on What You Know

A vision is easiest to create when you build on the principles we have discussed thus far:

1. *Connection.* By connecting with God and yourself, you can begin to paint a picture of what your ideal life looks like. You gain an understanding of who you are and why you are here. Once you identify your purpose, you have the foundation to create a vision that empowers you to fulfill it. Connecting with others will give you a broader perspective from which to shape your vision.

2. *Self-Curiosity.* The process of creating a vision often generates feelings of confusion, uncertainty, and doubt. As you dare to dream a bigger dream and paint that vivid and compelling vision, negative emotions can creep in to sabotage you. Self-curiosity will equip you to ask the questions that will help you turn emotional stumbling blocks into stepping stones for a vision that represents the true essence of your dreams.

people I knew in broadcasting. Within a few months I was a weekly contributor to the NBC affiliate in Dallas as well as two syndicated morning shows on ABC radio, serving as the resident life strategist. Then, as a result of a brief encounter, I was asked to co-host a television program called *The Potter's Touch* with Bishop T. D. Jakes. I had long read his best-selling books, watched him on Christian television, and recently joined his church, but I did not anticipate the opportunity to work with him in such a way. A bright and genuine woman who was assisting with the launch of the show—someone whom I had met just once and who had heard me speak for three minutes at an event—said she felt that God told her to call and ask me if I would be interested in the role as co-host.

The following year I created a daily sixty-second radio feature called *The Good Life,* which launched on thirty stations—all because of the power of connection with a fabulous producer whose show I'd appeared on as a guest. A year and a half later, the opportunity came to write for *Heart & Soul,* a women's lifestyle magazine. My monthly Q and A column called "Solve It" now reaches 1.5 million people. Opportunities continue to come my way, and I am blessed to be able to share my message through the power of media.

But none of this would have come about if I hadn't connected on all levels and continued to ask myself probing questions so that I could keep pursuing my vision.

IS YOUR VISION IMPAIRED?

As we have seen, there is no one way to fulfill your purpose in life. That is why we must be open to changes as they come our way and adjust our vision based on new experiences, opportunities, and circumstances. Your ability to create a clear and compelling vision will depend on how you process your life experiences. A lack of self-esteem and confidence as well as feelings of unworthiness can cloud your ability to see the possibilities for your life. By the same token, a healthy dose of self-esteem and confidence enables you to believe in your possibilities, exercise your faith, and ultimately watch the incredible path of your destiny unfold.

Your approach to life can affect three different aspects of your vision: perspective, perception, and focus. Perspective affects how you see yourself and your possibilities. Perception is determined by whether or not you are working with accurate information. And focus deals with how you spend your time and energy. Let's examine each of these more closely.

Perspective

Imagine for a moment that you have hiked a trail to the peak of a tremendous mountain. The majestic view of mountains, evergreen trees, and snowcaps in the distance literally takes your breath away. You can see roads, peaks, and valleys for miles. As you decide what path to hike back down the mountain, your viewpoint allows you to see all of your options and make the best decision before beginning your descent.

This type of viewpoint—the view from the top—also serves us well mentally. Unfortunately, many people never experience that viewpoint, which negatively impacts their perspective when they try to create a vision for their life.

A Limited Perspective

Do negative influences and relationships keep you from believing in your potential? Whether your parents were unsupportive or you've struggled with professional setbacks and failed relationships, the difficulties of life can knock you down so your perspective becomes too narrow. For example, if you are creating a vision on your path for a love relationship that helps you fulfill your life mission, but rejection or failed relationships continue to haunt you, your perspective will be limited by the past. Unless you gain a broader perspective, you won't be able to create a vision that satisfies your spirit.

The same holds true in every area of your life. If you are creating a vision of your business but don't truly believe you can succeed at a high level, your vision may be narrower than what is actually possible. Your vision for financial freedom can be restricted by past financial mistakes or a belief that you are incapable of handling money well. Your vision of career success can be impaired by worrying about a poor review, settling for a salary lower than what your contribution is worth, or buying into others' opinions of you.

When you are disconnected spiritually from God, emotionally from yourself, or socially from others, you lose perspective. Consider this extreme example: As I was speaking to a group of about twenty women at a domestic violence shelter, one of them sat quietly on the floor, listening intently but not showing any emotion. Two jet-black bruises below her eyes looked like war paint brushed across her small face. She was probably in her midforties, but her weary countenance made her appear a decade older. As I wrapped up my presentation, she timidly broke her silence.

"How do I make my life better when it's a mess? My family won't help me because he's threatened them after they've helped me before, and I've gone back to him. I didn't mean for him to go to jail," she said. "For the last two months, he kept me locked in our motel room while he went to work every day, and he unplugged the phone and took it with him. This time he accused me of being with another man while he was at work, and some people in the motel heard him beating me and called the police. I still love him though. I hope he's okay." I noticed several women leave the room at this point.

This broken woman was so disconnected from herself, her value, and her worth in God's eyes that her perspective was badly warped. "I went outside today, but I felt like I should call him to let him know what I was doing," she said at one point. Nothing I or any other woman in the group said registered in her mind.

When the discussion at the shelter ended that evening, a few of the women who had left the room returned and apologized. One of them explained, "It has taken a lot of therapy, prayer, and soul-searching for me to free myself from the abusive relationship I was in. I cannot afford to hear someone saying some of the ridiculous things I used to say when I was stuck in that trap." She was sensitive to the influence of other women's wrong attitudes on her progress.

This example may seem extreme, but something similar happens in our own lives when we connect with the wrong people and disconnect from God and ourselves. It can happen so gradually that you never notice until one day your sense of direction, purpose, and priorities are completely out of God's will for your life. When a person reaches this point, her mind needs to be completely renewed—often through professional counseling—before she is ready to create a fresh vision for life that expresses the potential God has placed within her.

Perhaps you have had debilitating experiences in your own life, such as physical or sexual abuse. Or perhaps your perspective has been affected by rejection, failure, or pain. What experiences in the following areas can impair your perspective and make it more challenging to believe in a larger vision of your life?

Spiritual Life:

Physical Health and Environments:

Relationships:

Work:

Finances and Resources:

Other:

These are real, everyday issues that you must deal with as you create your vision. Why? Because your vision must be big enough for you to clearly see that it is not something you can attain on your own. To come to fruition, a spirit-driven vision requires faith and divine help. As it begins to unfold, you will see evidence of opportunities that seemingly come out of nowhere. These types of occurrences confirm that you are on your path.

Changing Your Perspective

You can shift your perspective and improve your vision simply by making a decision to do so. The first step is to become aware that your perspective needs shifting. By acknowledging the ways in which your confidence has been shaken or your self-esteem has been damaged, you take the first step. Then you must recognize that through God you have the power to change your perspective.

Let's go back to the illustration of the magnificent mountain peak and the perfect viewpoint. Imagine for a moment that while hiking up the mountain, you are knocked down by a huge gust of wind. As you attempt to keep from falling, you trip over a small boulder and twist your ankle. When you finally make it near the mountaintop, you are too hurt to hike up to the best viewpoint. You are also too afraid to stand at the top for fear of being blown over again by a gust of wind. What if you fall again so close to the edge? So you get the best view you can, but not the view you need to make the best decision about the path to take down the mountain. And you never fully experience the breathtaking view from the top.

This is what happens to you when your fears, hurts, and failures keep you from moving forward and seeing the possibilities of life—let alone believing those possibilities can become reality. Divine intervention can remove the blinders so you can see from a healthy perspective. Through self-curiosity, you can explore your fears, hurts, and failures, and through connection with God, you can often resolve them.

The effects of my parents' separation when I was thirteen and their divorce when I was seventeen were not clear to me until I was in my twenties. Although the pattern was not obvious to me at the time, looking back I realize that I was too afraid of commitment and rejection to allow anyone into my life who *was* committed. So I rejected relationships that had promise and embraced ones that looked good from the outside but would not lead to marriage. Most of the time I steered clear of serious relationships altogether, which turned out to be a smart move. It ultimately helped me know myself better so that I could determine what was most important in a husband. I even created a list of twenty-eight qualities I sought in a mate and challenged myself to embody them. But it seemed no one ever came close to meeting my vision.

Although marriage was an important part of my life vision, I was not able to see that my perspective was putting my connection with the right person in jeopardy. As I grew in spiritual maturity, I began to pray a simple prayer:

Lord, show me where I am broken and tell me what I need to do to heal. I envision a relationship with a godly man whom I love and adore and who also loves and adores me. If it is not Your will for me to be married, I will accept that, but I believe in my spirit that it is. I trust that whoever he is, You are molding and shaping us both until we are ready for each other. Show me what I need to do to get ready.

Within a few weeks of that sincere prayer, I began to receive divine nudges and messages on television and from friends that spoke a similar theme to me: commitment. God was showing me where I was broken. I needed to increase my commitment to my work and open myself to the idea of truly committing to a relationship. Day by day God guided me to explore my feelings and take action despite my fears.

Around that time I began reconnecting with an incredible man named Charles to whom I had been engaged ten years earlier. We had called it off because the timing was not right, and we now lived two thousand miles apart with me in Dallas and him in Washington, D.C. I remained open to communicating with him although marriage was not on my mind. Then God began orchestrating a reunion. My father was involved with a project that required him to work in Washington, D.C., during the week. When I visited my father and later attended a speaking engagement, it was a perfect opportunity for Charles and me to reconnect. Not only was he still the handsome, thoughtful gentleman he had been before, but, like me, he had grown spiritually and personally. In fact, he possessed all twenty-eight qualities I had written down for my vision! The idea of committing still evoked a bit of fear, but I decided that my vision was more important than the fears that threatened to keep me from fulfilling it. Eleven years after his first proposal, Charles proposed a second time. I conquered the fears that limited my perspective and embraced marriage.

Viewing Life from God's Perspective

When you feel your perspective is off, forget *your* perspective altogether and imagine *God's* perspective. In fact, seek God's perspective daily. He has the master plan. He knows all of the possibilities and how He can use you if you are open to being His vessel. Step outside yourself for a moment and ask, How does God see my life? What is His viewpoint?

In 1 Samuel 16:7, God says, "For the LORD does not see as man sees; for man looks at the outward appearance, but the LORD looks at the heart." So often we tend to focus on our mistakes and failures, but God wants us to learn from them. Will you draw knowledge and wisdom from them to help you move forward on the unique path of your life, or will you continue to make the same mistakes time and again? That scripture also reminds us that we cannot fool God. He knows our motives, intentions, and truest desires. When you look at your life from His perspective, you seek truth, wisdom, and His will for your life. And your vision will be rooted in the same.

Invite God to transform your perspective. With His guidance, you can consciously make choices that support a healthier viewpoint about your abilities, talents, and possibilities. Often this means putting yourself in new environments and surrounding yourself with supportive people. It also means believing the wonderful things that God thinks about you.

Perception

When my mother suffered a stroke, one of the many effects was impaired vision. In addition to the dizziness that still plagues her, her depth perception was damaged. As a result, she had difficulty doing things like pouring a glass of water or touching her finger to her nose. Because I have had twenty-twenty vision my entire life, I never paid much attention to things like perception until a neurologist explained my mother's problem. Biologically, in order to have accurate depth perception, our eyes must be perfectly aligned. Our eyes work together to give us depth and distance perception. If we close one eye and attempt to go about our tasks, we'll find that we perceive many things to be closer or farther away than they really are.

Perception also plays a major role in creating a personal vision. Our perceptions are often assumptions that are based on untruths and incomplete information. Once the facts are obtained, our perceptions change. If we never obtain the facts, we can find ourselves creating a vision based on misinformation.

Christine is a client of mine whose vision involved starting a consulting practice, but she was reluctant to leave her existing job and give up her health insurance and 401(k) benefits. When I asked her the difference between the cost and coverage of her employer's insurance and any insurance she might purchase as a self-employed individual, she didn't know the answer. She hadn't looked into her insurance options and was relying instead on comments made by family members and friends, none of whom was self-employed. I asked if she had investigated any of the easy-to-start retirement plans available to entrepreneurs. Her answer, again, was no. I invited her to investigate her options, both for health care and retirement plans, and then continue creating her vision.

When Christine heard me say that I did not perceive health and 401(k) benefits to be serious obstacles to her vision for leaving her job to start a business, her perception began to change. As I shared my own experience with health insurance and retirement plans, she opened herself to my perception, which was based on personal experience rather than hearsay. When she acknowledged that millions of people have insurance and retirement plans without having an employer who shares the cost, her fears began to subside. After her research revealed that the costs were within reason for her, she was able to see just how close she was to bringing her vision to life.

You can improve your perception by opening yourself to hearing and considering the perception of others and educating yourself with the facts. Open yourself to learning what it will take to bring your vision to life. Remember the analogy of visual perception: If you close one eye, your perception becomes impaired. When you open both eyes, your perception is accurate. The same holds true with your personal vision. If you close yourself to learning and growth, your personal vision will become limited. If you open yourself to learning and growth, you can see the unlimited possibilities on your path.

Christine isn't the only person I know whose assumptions limited her vision. Michael, gifted with a rare combination of musical talents, found himself struggling with his vision when he discovered that family life was more important to him than a busy music career. In his mind, a successful career in music was synonymous with nonstop travel. He couldn't bear to be away from his wife and newborn baby for extended periods of time, so he couldn't see how to fulfill his purpose.

Knowing that he is a gifted songwriter, musician, and singer, I challenged Michael's assumption that the only opportunities for him in music involved performing at a hectic pace. We went through the process of creating a vision for his life that embraced his desire to be present in the lives of his wife and daughter, while providing an outlet for his passion and talent for music. As he considered his purpose of bringing people closer to God through his music, he identified his unique path. He created a vision that valued reaching people by performing at churches, conferences, and events. Acknowledging that fame and fortune were not priorities freed him to pursue a path that reflected his true values.

The first step to improving your perception is to identify areas in which your perception needs to be corrected. Like Michael, you have to be aware of assumptions that skew your perception. Rather than assuming that there is only one way for your vision to come alive, open yourself to a vision that is different from anything you have previously seen or known. Clarify your vision by asking questions that help you uncover your options. Rather than assuming you know the answers, think creatively and seek new ways of living your vision. Often, the greatest visions can be brought to life only through creativity and original thought. We will delve deeper into the concept of creativity in the next chapter.

Focus

The third aspect of vision is focus, which deals with how you spend your time and energy.

The Lord's Prayer says, "Give us this day our daily bread" (Matthew 6:11). This statement reminds us to focus on the task before us—not on tomorrow or next year, but on today. Having a powerful vision for your life makes it tempting to live in the future. But in order to bring the vision to fruition, you must be able to focus on the present and walk your path one day at a time. You need continual focus, along with consistent action, to bring your vision to life.

Think of managing your time and energy the way you think of managing money. The first step to taking control of your time and energy is to assess how you spend them. For one week, track how you spend your time each day. Then consider how you spent your time in light of the vision you have created. As you set priorities that will help you move toward that vision, determine to prune activities that no longer serve you in meaningful ways. Make room for your vision by clearing space in your schedule to focus on it.

Your stated intentions can be visionary, but if you spend your time distracted by things that do not support your intentions, you'll find yourself on a detour, heading away from your intended destination. The areas on which you focus your time and energy will expand, while areas starved of your time and energy will wither. How much time have you spent today working toward some aspect of your vision? How about this week? In the last month, how much time have you spent working toward your vision? If the bulk of your time was not spent acting on your vision, what did you spend your time doing?

The more you focus on your vision, taking deliberate steps on your divinely ordained path, the more opportunities and blessings will flow to you. If you choose instead to spend your time and energy on activities and aspects of life that don't fulfill your purpose, the opposite will happen. Many well-intentioned people have a powerful vision, but their actions have yet to reflect those thoughts. Their lives aren't moving toward their vision because they are spending their time and energy on the wrong things—things that don't propel them down their path.

Those who succeed in following their path take their gifts and talents to a higher level. Self-improvement takes time and energy. The temptation is to rest in your gifts and not hone your skills. Are you willing to build on the natural talents you possess? Are you willing to develop the discipline to improve day by day? By gaining control of your focus, you expand your vision and give it the attention it needs to come to life.

MAKING YOUR VISION A REALITY

Ecclesiastes 5:3 says, "A dream comes through much activity, and a fool's voice is known by his many words." If you are going to live your vision, you have to get busy! Stop talking about what you are going to do and just do it. In *Rich Minds, Rich Rewards,* I wrote about the importance of having a personal vision statement that illustrates how your life mission is fulfilled— and how to create a statement that is succinct and will move you to action.

When you create a personal vision for your life, it should clearly describe what you want most in life and include a time line and deadline for bringing the vision to fruition. A vision without a deadline is simply a dream.

A dream only serves us if we turn it into a vision and act on it to bring it to life. Otherwise, it only frustrates us and leaves us feeling hopeless and helpless. Most of us have told ourselves and those around us what we're going to do "one day." You might say, "One day I'm going to have my own business and work from home." Five years and two jobs later, you say, "One day I'm going to have my own business and work from home. I'm sick of the politics in the office and the rush-hour commute, and I have an idea for a business that I just know will do great. I wish I could quit my job and give it a try." Without a time line and a deadline for planning the business, making a smooth transition, and leaving your job, the idea remains an unfulfilled dream, and "one day" never comes.

A map with directions—an action plan—is the ideal tool for getting from point A to point B in life. Create an action plan to take you from where you are now to the realization of your vision. By listening and connecting introspectively and spiritually, you will be able to create a step-by-step action plan on a path to the life you were born to live.

As we will discuss in the chapter on "Expectancy," the action steps on your plan will make you a magnet for attracting opportunities and success with less effort than ever before. Your highest potential will come to life naturally, by trusting, acting, connecting, and moving forward on your path.

Deadlines Versus Time Lines

If you have a tendency to procrastinate, it is likely that you are very aware of deadlines. You know when a project needs to get done, but you do not follow a time line to get you from point A to point B. Instead, you wait until you are so close to the deadline that you must work frantically to meet it. Sound familiar? The solution for meeting your deadline is not focusing on the deadline, but instead, creating a plan with a time line. In order to set yourself up for success, it is imperative that you have a deadline and then break your vision into small, conceivable steps. Determine everything you will need to do to complete the project on time—and with excellence. Give each step its own deadline that supports your long-term deadline. Without a workable time line, a deadline can turn into a disaster. Moving from where you are now to the realization of your vision simply requires taking all of the steps necessary for you to get there.

Let's say, for example, that part of your vision is to dramatically improve your health in the next six months. Your first step would be to get specific about what that means. What would it mean to have your health dramatically improve? By being specific in your answer to create a measurable goal, you may decide that you will do the following:

- Lose thirty pounds.
- Exercise three times a week for at least thirty minutes.

- Stop drinking soft drinks and start drinking the recommended daily amount of water for your body weight.
- Adjust your schedule so that you get seven or more hours of sleep each night.
- Cut your consumption of red meat from five times a week to once a week.
- Eliminate fried foods from your diet, except on very special occasions (maybe once a month).

These are terrific goals, but if you attempt to do them all at once, you may find yourself overwhelmed. If you focus only on losing thirty pounds and then look in the mirror and see how heavy you are, you may never get started. So create a stairstep plan with benchmarks by which you can measure your progress.

Let's say that through self-curiosity, you realize that the reason you've never stuck to a weight-loss plan before is because you've identified the gym as the only place you can exercise and you've always made excuses about not having time to go. So you begin by implementing an exercise regimen that does not involve a gym. Next, you slowly cut back on your four soft drinks per day so that by your second or third week of exercise, you are drinking more water and just one soft drink per day. In the first week you eat red meat just three times, but by the fourth or fifth week, you are used to eating nonfried poultry and fish and eating red meat only once a week. You deliberately begin honoring your health and well-being by coming home earlier enough so that you have enough time to wind down, connect with the people who are important to you, and get to sleep at an hour that allows you to get the rest that will keep you refreshed (and looking great, too!). No more four- and five-hour nights—you have elevated your health standards.

By creating a time line with benchmarks by which you can measure your progress, you can focus less on the big task and the deadline and more on the small, incremental changes you are making.

Let God Set the Schedule

As you connect on a daily basis with God, yourself, and others, you will likely begin to clearly hear from God about the vision for your life. When this happens, don't hesitate to move forward. It's important to respond to His timing, even if it conflicts with your plan. By hesitating, you may miss blessings and opportunities that were designed just for you. Your job is to listen and move forward based on the direction He gives you when you connect with Him.

In a program for *The Potter's Touch,* I interviewed Bishop T. D. Jakes for a week-long series called "Living on Purpose." A minister, teacher, motivator, and author, Bishop Jakes had spent his entire life and ministry in West Virginia, but then he felt the Lord telling him to move his family and ministry to Dallas, Texas. He had no connection to Dallas other than its being "the place" the Lord told him to go. He was obedient and stepped out in faith. Within five years his church in Dallas had twenty-eight thousand members, and his ministry was growing exponentially and internationally.

Are you moving forward in response to God's instructions? If you wait for guarantees of future success, you may never step out in faith. You have no idea what God has in store for you until you are willing to move when He says move. Second Corinthians 5:7 tells us, "For we walk by faith, not by sight." As we continue walking our path and doing the work we are meant to do, we find that God creates a chain of opportunities that we might never have seen if we had not walked forward in faith.

Without the faith to step out of my career in public relations, I would not have had room in my life to take advantage of the opportunities that unfolded. Faith moved me to action, and action began bringing forth the vision. Like exercising a muscle, the more we exercise our faith, the stronger it becomes. As you build your faith muscles, you will find courage to allow

God's hand to guide you when you cannot see where your path is taking you. You simply trust the sweet-smelling aroma of your destiny that lets you know you are moving in the right direction.

In the next chapter we'll discuss how creativity can stretch your mind and imagination so that you can respond to these God-given opportunities in ways you have never before considered.

❧ WALKING YOUR PATH ❧

Listen to Your Life: How Clear Is Your Vision?

Place a check mark in front of every statement that is true for you.

____ Making a decision about what I want to do with my life comes easily for me.

____ I have a written vision statement of what my ideal life looks like.

____ When I discover an opportunity that fulfills my purpose and vision, I pursue it with passion, which leads to even greater opportunities.

____ I learn from, but don't beat myself up for, past mistakes or failures.

____ I do not compare my circumstances with other people's.

____ I am actively moving toward my vision on a daily basis.

____ After reading this chapter, I realize that my perspective on life is a "view from the top."

____ The vision I have created is one that I cannot accomplish if I stay within the parameters of my current comfort zone. I will have to step out in faith or it won't happen!

____ I have a deadline by which I would like to achieve my goals.

____ Once I set goals, I remain focused until I accomplish them.

____ I do not feel stuck in any way.

If you could not check off all of the above statements, it is important to make a plan to create a clearer vision of your life and take the necessary steps to overcome the fear that may be keeping you from following your plan.

5-Minute Action Step

Carve out five minutes today and identify what is preventing you from creating a clear, compelling vision for your life. Perhaps you are afraid of repeating a past failure. Or maybe you have been focusing on a vision that does not express the essence of who you are. Listen to your life and identify the challenges you face as you embark on the process of creating a vision. Identifying challenges is the first step to overcoming them. List the first five here. If needed, continue on another piece of paper or in your journal.

1.

2.

3.

4.

5.

48-Hour Challenge

During the next two days, listen for God's guidance and write a clear and compelling personal vision statement. This vision statement will enable you to define what extraordinary success looks like to you. By defining success for yourself, you give yourself a target to aim for. Be sure your definition includes a date by which you plan to be living your vision. Remember, success is more likely when you are specific about what you want *and* you set a deadline. Create a time line to support your deadline and start moving! If you do not have a journal, write your vision statement here:

❧ Prayer of Vision ❧

Today, God, I ask You to restore my sight just as Jesus did for so many during His life. Show me the vision You have for my life. Expand my vision beyond my comfort zone. I believe that You are able to do exceedingly abundantly above all that I could ever ask or think, according to the power that works within me. Ephesians 3:20 *Plant a vision in my spirit that reflects Your divine purpose for me. Help me see clearly as I walk on my path. Open my eyes to blind areas in my life and to everything that will enable me to grow and fulfill my purpose. Grant me wisdom and strength to gracefully handle those things that are unpleasant or difficult to see, and give me the strength to face the issues that ultimately impair my vision. Perfect my perspective on life, my perception of reality, and my ability to focus on my vision despite distractions, trials, and challenges. Your Word says that "where there is no vision, the people perish."* Proverbs 29:18, KJV *I do not want to walk aimlessly through life, pursuing hollow dreams. I pray for the ability to listen to my life so that I can write the vision, make it plain, and boldly walk toward it. Amen.*

CREATIVITY

Stretching Your Mind to Explore All Your Options

In order to have what you have never had,
you must be willing to do what you have never done.
—LES BROWN

In the late 1970s, Art Fry was sitting in church choir practice, frustrated because the scraps of paper he used to mark his hymnal kept falling out. The problem was certainly not new, but on this particular day, he had an idea for a solution. He worked in the retail tape division of his employer, 3M, and had been trying to figure out what to do with a new, low-tack adhesive invented by another employee, Dr. Spencer Silver. Fry's idea was so simple, yet so creative, that hearing it makes you say, "Why didn't *I* think of that?" Today, his concept, the Post-it note, is a multimillion dollar product that can be found in nearly every office—and most homes—in America.

Like the Post-it note, some of the most creative ideas are born of problems that need solutions.

When we talk about creativity and creative people, we tend to think of artists, writers, musicians, and performers. However, I'd like to suggest that you think of creativity in a more creative way. Let me give you some examples: The exceptional teacher who has a knack for teaching children who had previously been labeled "learning disabled" is tapping into the spirit of creativity. The husband who manages to keep romance alive with his wife through thoughtfulness and surprises has adopted the practice of creativity. The entrepreneur who manages to generate buzz about her product to beef up sales on a shoestring marketing budget is employing the principle of creativity. And so is the stay-at-home mom who homeschools her children, providing them with fresh challenges and nurturing their enthusiasm for learning.

By shifting to a broader definition of creativity, we can all begin to see our creative talents—and appreciate them.

WALKING THE PATH OF CREATIVITY

Creativity is the ability to bring to life something of purpose, value, and appeal that did not previously exist. With this definition, we are able to apply the principle of creativity to all areas of life—from artistic endeavors to business objectives, from our relationships to our spiritual lives. Creativity is about *creating* something. Whether you are creating a business, a project, a song, a loving relationship, a healthier body, a movie, a book, a home, an independent life, a career, a new look, or a cure for cancer, tapping into the power of creativity will release your previously undeveloped ideas and talents.

Just as an artist begins with a blank canvas and through the flow of creativity—a process many artists describe as spiritual—creates a masterpiece, so you, too, can paint a masterpiece on the canvas of your life.

Some of the most fruitful and satisfying paths are often the most creative. Those who have found a way to think and act creatively usually find success. Their creative ideas revolutionize entire industries, transform lives, and influence societal values.

Pursuing Innovation

We are often discouraged from pursuing things that are new and different because we are afraid that our ideas may fail. We need only look to companies that have successfully introduced new, over-the-top concepts to see that it's possible to build something from nothing.

As a college student at Yale University, Frederick W. Smith earned a C on a now-famous paper about a creative idea: nationwide overnight delivery service. Undaunted by his grade, Smith later set out to create a national overnight delivery service in 1971. He devised a creative system in which packages would be picked up from their respective locations, flown to a hub in Memphis, Tennessee, sorted at night, flown to their destinations, and delivered by truck to customers' doorsteps the following day. Federal Express, as Smith named his brainchild, began service to twenty-five cities with fourteen jets in 1973. Such a concept had never been attempted on a national scale, and many considered it unnecessary at the time. The critics underestimated the demand. Today, overnight delivery is considered a necessity in the business world. FedEx delivers five million packages each business day. And other organizations, from United Parcel Service to the United States Postal Service, have followed suit in providing overnight delivery.

"There are two keys to innovation," Smith wrote in *Fast Company* magazine in 2000. "The first is the ability to think beyond relatively conventional paradigms and to examine traditional constraints using nontraditional thinking. You have to be able to go outside your own frame of reference and find another way to look at a problem. The second key to innovation is the ability to discern the important issues and to keep your real goal in view."[1]

In others words, you need to look at your challenges from a different perspective and maintain your focus on the long-term vision despite the distractions you encounter. Too often, people consider only the most obvious path to their vision, but innovative thinking and an open mind will lead you to explore all options that may better enable you to accomplish the end result.

Blazing Trails for Others to Follow

Numerous options exist to move you from point A to point B on your path. Some options will fit like exquisitely tailored garments, while others simply don't feel right. At times all doors to your innermost desires will seem closed. This is when your creativity is most valuable. It takes conviction and an inner certainty of your destiny to create opportunities in the face of adversity. From these necessary creative endeavors, we often discover a lesson or a gift that reaps benefits beyond our own personal satisfaction. When you create something from nothing because no other option exists for traveling the path you were born to live, you will find yourself thrust into the leadership role of a pathfinder or trailblazer.

When I was employed as a marketing director, I had the opportunity to create events that would enable my employer to raise our firm's visibility in the business community. In 1996, I came up with the idea of presenting an award each year to one woman who had blazed trails in business or the community. I named it the Texas Trailblazer Award. For me the greatest treat at the annual luncheon was meeting the amazingly creative, bold, and pioneering women. Let me introduce you to a few:

---

1. Frederick W. Smith, quoted in Jill Rosenfield, *Fast Company*, no. 33 (April 2000): 97.

- Louise Raggio is an eighty-something attorney who led the fight to pass a law in 1967 that allowed Texas women to own property, obtain bank loans, and own their own businesses without the signature of a husband or father. It wasn't an easily won fight, but Louise was on a mission and never gave up.
- Ebby Halliday is the founder of a company that sells over one billion dollars' worth of homes each year, making it one of the largest privately owned residential real estate companies in the United States. The ultimate saleswoman, she founded the company in 1945, a time when very few women were running businesses.
- Nancy Brinker, in honor of her younger sister who didn't survive the disease, founded the Susan G. Komen Foundation to help fight breast cancer. She created something from nothing, and so far has raised nearly $600 million for research.
- Anita N. Martinez, with her assertive, energetic style, is another of the inspiring recipients. In the late 1960s, her successful grass-roots campaign led her to become the first Hispanic woman elected to a major U.S. city council.

All of these women saw opportunities to do things that had never been done before and, with creativity and vision, blazed trails in a major way.

Relandscaping as You Go

In 2002, Lauren Hutton—often called the world's first supermodel—was a special guest at the annual Trailblazer event and presented the award. I knew of her modeling and acting endeavors, and I'd heard about her recent near-fatal motorcycle crash, but it wasn't until I had the opportunity to chat with her that I realized how her spirit of creativity had revolutionized the modeling world in the mid-1970s. Her story is an inspiration to anyone who doubts the power of one creative idea.

When Lauren Hutton headed to New York in the early 1960s, she was looking for a way to finance her dream of traveling to Africa. She soon stumbled into a profession that paid women, as she told me, "a dollar a minute." Within her first year of modeling, she was headed to Paris to shoot with the most coveted cover in modeling: *Vogue* magazine. Since

What Your Life Is Saying About Creativity

How do you know when you need to tap into your own creativity?

- You feel that you do not have any options, or your options are very limited.
- You are afraid to try new ideas or new ways of doing things.
- You have limited yourself to one way of accomplishing your vision.
- Life feels boring, stale, or uneventful.
- You never ask, Why can't it be done another way? about anything.
- You play it safe in most situations.
- You are uncomfortable leading others and almost always prefer to follow someone else's lead.

How do you know when your creativity is actively and positively impacting your vision?

- You often create new ideas, new products or services, or new ways of doing what you do.
- People come to you because of your problem-solving abilities.
- Life is an exciting, interesting adventure.
- You embrace new ideas and concepts, or you at least open your mind to learning about them.
- You know the joy of creating something from nothing.
- You don't mind standing out in a crowd or being different from others.
- You consistently focus on and take action toward your vision.

then she has appeared on the cover of *Vogue* more often than anyone else; the millennium issue of *Vogue* marked her twenty-eighth cover.

In 1974, after ten years as one of most well-known models in the world, Lauren pioneered a creative concept that literally changed the land-scape of the modeling profession and made her the world's first super-model. It occurred to her that models should not be paid by the hour, but according to the value of the service they were providing. From that thought, she made the bold move of asking for an exclusive contract that paid her based on the sales power of her name and face. Lauren negotiated the first-ever exclusive modeling contract and signed a seven-figure deal with Revlon that year. Lauren Hutton blazed the trail, and within months, other models followed in her footsteps. After her historic feat, modeling fees grew from hundreds to hundreds of thousands, and the modeling industry changed from a mom-and-pop business into a multimillion-dollar industry. In 1974, New York City was home to just five modeling agencies. One year later it boasted more than thirty agencies.

Lauren remained the face of Revlon until the age of forty-six, proving that twenty-somethings aren't the only ones who can move products and open doors for models over the age of twenty-five who were previously considered "past their prime."

Her popularity allowed her to transition into acting. She has appeared in more than thirty films, costarring with such actors as Richard Gere, Robert Redford, and Jim Carey. In 1996 and 1997, she hosted her own late-night talk show in New York and Los Angeles, and her life has been chronicled by Lifetime, NBC, and E! Entertainment. Incidentally, she *was* able to finance her dream of traveling to Africa; to date she has visited the continent twenty-seven times.

Creativity combined with business sense and boldness have ensured Lauren Hutton's place in the history of modeling.

Your vision may not call for you to come up with a multimillion-dollar idea or change the face of an industry. You may define success as raising well-educated and well-rounded children, building a joyful marriage, or achieving a debt-free lifestyle. Creativity is an important tool for reaching these visions too. By exploring options other than the obvious, you may end up spearheading a grass-roots effort to improve the quality of education in your children's school, for example. The idea is rooted in your desire for better schools for your own children, but ultimately your creative ideas will benefit so many more.

In this chapter we'll look at how to nurture a spirit of creativity, break free from rules and roles, resist the fear that drains us of creative energy, and gain the courage to explore.

Nurturing a Spirit of Creativity

God has placed within each of us all the creativity we need for our journey. Our job is to tap into it. The more you connect with your spirit, the easier creativity becomes. Remember, everything that has ever been brought into existence began with a thought. The neighborhood you live in was nothing more than a piece of land until someone thought to turn it into something more. Every company, from Microsoft to Starbucks, began as nothing more than a thought. The clothes you're wearing right now were once a mere thought. You—yes, you!—were brought into existence because of a thought in the minds of your parents.

Thoughts when joined with creativity produce the actions that bring something into existence out of nothing. The God-given gift of creativity has allowed the human race to make great progress in areas such as science and technology. Imagine how your life might be different if innovators hadn't been curious enough to ask, "What if we could fly?" "What if we could talk to people thousands of miles away through a wire that transmits sound?" "What if every computer could be connected to a common network that allows for the sharing of information?" "What if we didn't need to rely on animals for transportation?" Countless acts of creativity shape the way we live every day.

So how can you generate creative thoughts? One of the best ways is through self-curiosity. People with inquisitive minds question everything and are consistently seeking new ways to use their talents and gifts, overcome obstacles, and improve upon what already exists.

Several years ago I asked myself, What if I could work from anywhere I wanted to live? The question intrigued me, and it also helped shape my vision for a life in which I could have more control over my time. I did not like driving in traffic. I thought I might want to move to another city within a few years, but I also recognized the difficulty of moving a locally focused business to a new city. Although I was single at the time, I knew I would eventually want the flexibility of being at home more. The simple question, What if I could work from anywhere I want to live? helped confirm a path that involved coaching, writing, and speaking—all of which can be done from anywhere I want to live.

List some what-if questions that could spark creativity and make your vision come alive. Think of five vision-driven questions to get your creative juices flowing:

1.
2.
3.
4.
5.

In addition to employing self-curiosity, we can take any number of steps to put the power of creativity to work in our lives, including opening up our imaginations, surrendering to divine inspiration, making opportunities to change our perspective, summoning the willpower to give something new a try, and connecting with people who can help us process our ideas.

Let Your Imagination Run Free

Gabriella is the adorable but fiercely independent five-year-old daughter of some close family friends. "Gabby," as we call her, is also a fantastic story-teller. Before I knew better, I would listen to her stories and ask questions, which she would answer in vivid detail. She once went into elaborate detail about how she and her family were going to Cancun, Mexico. She told me who was going, when they were going, and what they would do when they got there. She made it sound quite exciting and then asked if I would consider going with them. When I mentioned to her parents that Gabby had taken the liberty of inviting me to join them on their vacation, they looked at me oddly. "Cancun? We're not going to Cancun." They had no idea what I was talking about! I still listen to her fabulous stories, but with a bit more laughter and friendly skepticism.

Gabby's imagination created a vision of something that sounded fun and adventurous. Her imagination was apparently sparked by a photograph of a beautiful beach in Cancun that she saw in a photo album of mine. She allowed herself to imagine that she could go there too.

Most of us could use some of that childlike imagination in our own lives. One way to fuel creativity is by exposing yourself to new ideas constantly. Fill your life with inspiration by stocking your mind with images that trigger your imagination, just as the beach photograph sparked Gabby's. Read books that focus on areas aligned with your vision. Immerse yourself in activities that support your vision and allow you to see images, people, and environments that give you a fresh perspective. By constantly exposing yourself to this type of inspiration, you keep your passion alive and expand your thoughts.

Connect with Divine Inspiration

God is the Master of creativity. By connecting with the Creator, we tap into the most powerful source of creativity. Just consider the world around you—the sky, the sun, the water that gives life to plants and animals and us, the changing seasons, the countless varieties of animals, and the multitude of cultures and languages and countries. Consider that of the six billion people on earth, no two are the same. Even identical twins are not completely identical! Indeed, it appears that God immensely enjoys creativity. He has fun with it—and we can too. As beings created in His image, we have creativity within us. And when we surrender our lives to His care, His divine creativity can be expressed through us.

When you are on a spiritual path, sometimes the challenge is remembering that you don't have to do all of the work by yourself. God is waiting for you to ask for help. Lay your desires before Him and simply ask, *How should I go about this?* Then listen for His wisdom and guidance through the leading of the Holy Spirit.

God's way of working through us is to give us a spirit of creativity. That is why you often hear artists and writers talk about experiencing a "flow" in which they did not even feel that they were doing the work, but rather were being used as vessels to produce the work.

Schedule Time to Be Inspired

Inspiration for creativity is all around us. For me, spending time in nature is a catalyst for creative inspiration. When I go outside and take a walk, I connect with God. The sights and sounds of nature awaken my senses to the wealth of creativity evident all around me. At times I purposely connect with nature to fuel my creative flow.

While hiking with a friend to the top of Cathedral Rock in Sedona, Arizona, I stopped to take a break and absorb the beauty of the moment. I sat in the middle of what once must have been an impressive and dramatic waterfall. No water remains, only streaks where water ran over the bold, red rocks that cascade down the side of the mountain. The only sound was the wind brushing past me, and my eyes were captivated with a vivid and spectacular view that I can only describe as coming from the hand of the Divine. I savored the moment in quiet meditation.

I returned from Arizona inspired and full of ideas. I also made a conscious decision to schedule more time in my life to enjoy nature and places with natural beauty, a joy that has always resonated with my spirit but not necessarily with my schedule.

All of us can schedule inspiration from time to time by identifying what inspires us and then taking time to do it.

What three activities inspire you most?

Whether it's reading a book about someone whose life or ideas invigorate you, playing with children, or taking an adventurous vacation, determine what gets your creativity going. Then schedule time to do it.

Choose to Stretch Yourself

Although it is helpful to *feel* inspired, it is not a necessity for creativity. Julia Cameron, author of *The Artist's Way* and *The Right to Write*, suggests that writers "prime the pump." In other words, rather than waiting for inspiration to hit, writers should simply begin writing without regard to how "good" the writing is. Once a writer gets going, the inspiration will come. One idea leads to the next, and before you know it, the writing is flowing.

The same holds true for creativity in any area of life. If you are having difficulty connecting with your creative spirit, begin by identifying a challenge for which you would like a creative solution. Make a list of ideas, regardless of how ridiculous they may seem. As you think through each idea, one will inevitably spark another until, eventually, you have an idea that excites you. The goal is to allow yourself to get lost in the process. Imagine the possibilities. Play with ideas. Have fun! Whether you are a sales executive or a musician, creativity—the ability to bring to life something of purpose, value, and appeal that did not previously exist—will stretch your mind and allow you to consider all options.

Creativity is not about the end result as much as it is about stretching our minds and considering all options. Focusing exclusively on the end result is a sure way to get stuck in a rut. The pressure to produce creates anxiety, which restricts the flow of ideas and the ability to fully use our imaginations. Even creatively gifted people can get stuck in a rut if they continually rely on their past creativity.

If you lack confidence in your creativity, begin with something you perceive as low risk. Let's say that part of your vision is being promoted within your company, but you have been struggling to perform at your full potential. You will want to be creative as you seek ways to improve your performance at work. Begin generating ideas and see where they lead. And don't be afraid to ask other people for input.

Connect Creatively with Others
Creativity doesn't have to be a solo endeavor. The best creative ideas often come when we connect with other people to get other points of view.

Often a fresh perspective gives us just the edge we need to generate an incredible idea that feeds into our vision.

Sometimes all you need is to verbalize your creativity with a trusted confidant. By talking about it and getting encouragement, you gain the confidence you need to move forward. When you talk about your creative ideas with someone you trust, you validate your creativity, and the perspective of another person can add depth and new meaning to your project. Connecting with others can enable you to receive affirmation for your ideas while also strengthening them.

While I was writing this book, my creativity was enriched by sharing and listening to the perspectives of others. I occasionally shared the principles I was developing with several people whose wisdom and opinions I value. Their enthusiasm, sense of intrigue, and immediate understanding of the principles let me know that I was indeed on the right path. As I described each principle, listeners frequently offered an example of how they had experienced some aspect of it in their own lives. Then something even more wonderful would happen. They would point out an aspect of the principle that I had not yet considered. They deepened my perspective on my creative endeavor.

In chapter 1, I shared a story about the chain of events that led to the creation of Cathleen Whitelow Jewels. She told that story after I shared my thoughts on the principle of connection with the women having brunch that morning. She immediately related to the principle because she had seen how it shaped the path of her own life.

Remember, God often speaks to us through people. We can connect with others we know, or we can connect by looking to examples of those whose endeavors are similar to our vision. Why waste creativity and energy reinventing the wheel when you could use them to improve upon existing ideas? Make a habit of taking interest in the success path of those whom you admire. Take note of their perseverance, the obstacles they overcame, and their big breaks. By doing this, you can prevent yourself from tripping over similar obstacles on your path, and you'll find role models to help you move beyond the things that box you in and limit your creative thinking.

STEPPING OUT OF ROLES AND RULES

Even as we put tools such as imagination and connection to work, our creative thinking can be blocked by the roles we have become accustomed to playing or by the rules we're playing by.

Many people feel stifled in their creativity because their spirit is buried beneath a host of labels: "teacher," "nurse," "engineer," "businessperson," "employee," "parent," "husband," "wife." Then we define ourselves with descriptive labels—race, religious denomination, where we live, what we drive, whom we know, and so forth. Personality descriptors also affect our beliefs about our own creativity, as they become self-fulfilling prophecies. If you have always been told that you are gifted, creative, and adventurous, you are likely to live up to those descriptions because you have come to believe them. By the same token, if you have always been told that you are technical, practical, or average, you are likely to live up to those personality descriptors. Then when someone suggests that you have creative abilities, you react with "Oh no! I've never been the creative type."

Look at your vision for your life and ask yourself, What's the best way for me to get from here to there? Consider the traditional routes; they may be sufficient. But if you find yourself constantly bumping into obstacles, ask yourself, What options have I yet to consider?

Creativity also involves freeing ourselves from the rules that box us in. Have you ever played a game with a young child? If so, you know that following the rules to the letter isn't as much fun as watching children come up with their own ideas for how to play. Eventually, of course, the older people in their lives usually corral that creativity so the game can be played "as it was meant to be," but something of that creative spark is lost along the way.

Children are naturally creative. One of their most precious traits is that they are not limited by small thinking. Ask some children what they'd like to be when they grow up, and they may answer, "I wanna be an architect and a baseball player" or "I want to be an actress and a choreographer" or "Well, first, I want to make a hundred million dollars playing basketball, and then I'm going to have my own company." Children believe anything is possible. They are full of dreams and optimism.

Between childhood and adulthood, something changes for most people. The realities of day-to-day living begin to bury not only the creative ideas but the possibilities for a life of purpose, passion, and joy. Before you know it, years have passed and your dreams are buried so deep that you sometimes forget you ever had them. At some point between adolescence and young adulthood, many minds become deprogrammed from believing that anything is possible.

Sadly, the crushing of our creative spirit and the power of imagination begins when we are children. The adults in our lives, believing they are doing us a favor, give us a dose of reality by discouraging us from pursuing a life that seems too grand. "Now, baby," a mother may say, "your writing is good, but it's probably not going to pay the bills. You need to pursue something that's in demand. How about teaching English or writing copy for an ad agency? That's a more realistic use of your talent." Our spirits are saddened to hear this news, perhaps even angered by the lack of support for our authentic dreams. For a while we may ignore the naysayers, but eventually, at the slightest obstacle or perceived failure, we adopt the same attitude. We feed our minds the junk food of negativity, self-doubt, and fear rather than a nourishing diet of vision, purpose, and encouragement. Often we embrace the same think-*inside*-the-box rules as the people who discouraged us.

Depending on who raised you and how they raised you, the rules may have begun to stifle your creativity as early as your toddler years. If not, the rules definitely began to take over when you entered school. School is where we learn how things are and are not supposed to be done. School is where everything is either right or wrong and there is rarely any room in between, unless you are blessed with a creative teacher in a creative subject. Curiosity and creativity are not generally encouraged in traditional education, and so for twelve to twenty years, you learn that following the rules is rewarded with success.

Of course, rules and order serve a purpose, often a very good purpose. However, when it comes to walking your unique path, success often comes as a result of not doing things the way they have always been done. Success results from following your spirit, even when doing so makes no sense to anyone else. Creativity requires a consistent practice of doing things just a little bit differently—not simply for the sake of being different, but because that is what your path calls for and because you are following a divine plan.

As a teenager, I imagined owning my own company. I didn't know what kind of company it would be, but I liked the idea of working for myself. After college and graduate school, my plan had been to work for six or seven years, get a variety of experience, and then venture out to start my own business. But the opportunity came sooner than expected. I was employed full time for less than two years when I had the opportunity to start my own public relations agency. The rules would have dictated that I work for a public relations agency before starting one of my own. The rules would have kept me from answering the door when opportunity knocked. It was not in my plan to do so quite this soon in my life, but I took advantage of it. My path called for it. And in fact, my plan for waiting seven or eight years would have been in direct conflict with God's plan of using me to do what I do now.

Learn to be more sensitive to your unique path than you are to rules, especially when unique blessings and opportunities arise. This is essential if you're to conquer the greatest challenge to creativity: fear.

RESISTING THE SPIRIT OF FEAR

When it comes to embracing new ideas for your life, you can expect to feel fear. Whenever you have a great idea, fear loves to squash it. The spirits of fear, failure, and mediocrity point out everything you have ever done wrong or regretted. They work overtime building a case against you, all the while convincing you that they are working in your best interest—after all, you don't want to make a fool of yourself or waste your time or money. A spirit of fear is a spirit devoid of faith, because fear is based in past experience rather than on future possibilities. A spirit of fear says that what has happened in the past will always happen.

But fear only has as much power as you give it. The past, whether filled with failure or success, does not determine your future—unless you allow it to do so. You can choose to operate in a spirit of fear, or you can choose to reject it, even if you have lived your entire live in fear, failure, and mediocrity.

Facing the Questions of Fear

Fear often comes in the form of negative questions. Unlike the empowering questions that spark creativity, such as "What if I could do my work from anywhere I live?" these what-if questions are intended to intimidate you. "What if it doesn't work?" "What if I fail?" or "What if it's a bad idea?" The way to overcome this sometimes persistent block to creativity is to answer your own doubts and fears. By doing so, you realize that *if* you fail, it won't be the end of the world, and most likely, the risk of failure is worth the risk that you might just succeed!

Just as the spirit of fear fights to dominate your thoughts, the spirit of success vies for your attention and trust. The spirit within you connects with God and understands your purpose and your highest potential. It is a spirit based in faith that great things are in store.

Ephesians 3:20 says, "To Him who is able to do exceedingly abundantly above all that we ask or think, according to the power that works in us." God, the Author of all creativity, is the power working in you. But to connect with His power, you must first acknowledge that it is available to you. In prayer, ask for the creativity to think beyond the invisible boundaries you have set for yourself. And ask for courage to fearlessly embrace that creativity in the fulfillment of your vision. In Joshua 1:6,9 and Deuteronomy 31:6, God commands us to "be strong and of good courage." In Psalm 27:14, He encourages us again, "Wait on the LORD; be of good courage, and He shall strengthen your heart; wait, I say, on the LORD!"

Overcoming the Fear of the Unknown

Creativity leads us into unknown territory—and one of our most prevalent fears is fear of the unknown. Creativity, by definition, extends beyond the status quo. It is different, and therefore often finds itself under criticism. The spirit of fear speaks up to remind you of why your creative ideas are bad ones. In your mind, it will sound something like this:

- *That's a stupid idea. What on earth makes you think that will work?*

- *You can't do that. You are not smart enough, good enough, attractive enough, experienced enough, old enough, young enough, wealthy enough...*
- *No one has ever done that before. I don't know what makes you think you can.*
- *Remember the last time you came up with an idea and it failed? Wasn't it embarrassing? Remember? Do you want to go through that again?*
- *What if you fail? It's better to play it safe. That way you won't look bad.*
- *Who do you think you are to do that? You're not anybody special. Stop dreaming!*
- *You're the underdog. How are you going to compete without getting trampled?*

When we experience these kinds of doubts about moving forward with our creative ideas, we must not back down. Instead, stand up for what you know in your spirit. Once you succeed, you'll see that your inner critics quiet down and sometimes even start supporting you.

Moving Forward in Fearlessness

Fear produces not only doubt but also hesitation. When we hesitate to move forward on a spiritual nudge, we risk missing an opportunity that was meant for us. Moving forward on your creative ideas is an act of faith.

Fearless mountain climber William Hutchinson Murray said it so well: "Concerning all acts of initiative or creation, there is one elementary truth, the ignorance of which kills countless ideas and splendid plans: that the moment one definitely commits oneself, then Providence moves too."[2]

The last three words are the key. "Providence moves too." Providence

---

2. W. H. Murray, *The Scottish Himalaya Expedition* (1951).

is God. Once you move, God moves, putting things in place and using your own creativity to bless your endeavors.

Hesitation can cause missed opportunities because none of us has the privilege of seeing the divine order of God's universe and how things are lining up to cross our path until we move forward. When you hesitate, you risk missing out on a blessing or opportunity that may cross your path because you have not taken the steps that will lead you to the right place to receive it. Similarly, moving too soon or pushing something to happen out of fear can have the same effect. Instead of not being far enough along to be in position for an opportunity, you have sprinted down the path when you should have been jogging. Have you ever felt as if you were in overdrive, trying without success to make everything come together? It is important to distinguish between fear that stems from your ego and the uneasiness or lack of peace that is a signal from God.

Remember that the vision God gives us is only a glimpse of a greater plan. Your creativity serves the purpose of moving you closer to your vision. Once you move closer, you see how your vision is intertwined with a greater plan, one that often involves more than just you.

When I presented the idea for the Texas Trailblazer Award to my employer in 1996 and received the go-ahead to produce the event, I had no idea of the ways in which the annual luncheon would impact my life. In fact, I had no idea it would even become an annual event. I can trace countless opportunities back to that event. In addition to raising more than $250,000 thus far for The Family Place, a domestic violence shelter and resource center, the event paved the way for connections that led to meeting new friends, new clients, and even the opportunity to co-host *The Potter's Touch* television program. In fact, through one of that program's guests, former BET news-anchor-turned-speaker Cheryl Martin, the proposal for this book landed on the desk of my publisher! Other people have made significant connections through the event as well. Jobs have been won. Awareness and understanding of domestic violence has been increased. Relationships have been forged. By listening to my spirit when the creative idea came to me, "Providence moved."

What creative idea are you hesitant about?

When God tells you to move forward, do it. At such times you must simply let go of the past and focus on the present. Look that spirit of fear in the face and say, "You will not control my actions any longer." That's fearlessness. Creativity thrives on it. Recognize that fear is not of God: "God has not given us a spirit of fear, but of power and of love and of a sound mind" (2 Timothy 1:7).

GAINING THE COURAGE TO EXPLORE

As I was writing this afternoon, I received a call from my cousin Javon, who is a playwright. Javon is always writing and is very determined to succeed. He has learned to continually focus and consistently act on his vision of being a successful writer. He was not born with any particular advantages, but he discovered his love for writing while following his passion to act. That passion led him to continue his education after graduating from South Carolina State University. While earning a master's degree in theater at the University of Pittsburgh, he decided to try writing a play of his own. It was a hit! He discovered that his love for acting did not match his passion for writing stories. Now, at twenty-nine years old, he has written twelve stage plays and a screenplay. His work has been featured at the Sundance Festival, in *USA Today,* the *Chicago Tribune,* and on MSNBC. His plays have been performed in Los Angeles, New York, Chicago, Washington, D.C., Atlanta, Philadelphia, and numerous other cities around the country. He called for no particular reason this afternoon except to ask how I've been doing.

After I brought him up to speed on my life, I asked, "What are you up to?" He casually responded that he is finishing a play for husband-and-wife R&B singers Kenny Lattimore and Chanté Moore.

"Really?!" I replied. It sounded pretty exciting to me.

"Yes," he replied. "It will tour in ten cities starting next month."

I began thinking of how hard and consistently Javon has worked since we were in college, even during the times when he struggled to make it. He never stops moving forward. Although he had not called me to talk about creativity and potential, I thought I'd get his insight on the subject.

"What do you think keeps people from fulfilling their potential?" I asked.

"Many people don't have the courage to explore their potential," he replied. "They don't acknowledge their own talent. They don't see it as valid. Because they are critical of themselves, they never move forward."

"So you think there are many good writers out there who simply don't think they are 'good enough' to pursue what they are passionate about?" I asked.

"Exactly. And even if they pick up a pen and write, they are afraid to let anyone read it, so their efforts stop there," he explained.

"So what drives you to fulfill your highest potential?" I probed.

"The love of what I do and the prospect of being successful at it," he told me.

As I coach individuals and read mail from readers of my column, I'm amazed to see how complicated many people believe it is to achieve success at what they are naturally gifted to do. Because they believe it is difficult, they never truly explore the possibilities. Their fear that the possibilities are not really attainable keeps them from moving forward. Heed Javon Johnson's advice: Have the courage to explore.

Exploration does not mean you are committing to anything. It simply means you are having fun with your talent and considering where it could lead. Play with it. No obligation. Simply enjoy exploring. When you do something out of sheer exploration, you have the courage to go places you might not otherwise go.

When you take steps on your path, pulled forward by a compelling vision, it will not always be obvious which direction to take. Sometimes there are multiple choices and no one right way to do what needs to be done. What could you explore today that you have pondered for years? What potential have you glimpsed but never delved into? What talents could you play with? Perhaps you want to explore song writing, entrepreneurship, or real estate investing. What possibilities could you explore in your relationships? Could you explore forgiveness or patience? Just try it and see what it feels like. To explore more options to bring your vision to life, consider these important steps:

1. Notice the emotions you feel regarding a particular issue. Do you feel apprehension? fear? inadequacy? frustration?

2. Close your eyes and imagine what it would be like to feel the opposite of those emotions. So instead of fear, you imagine feeling courage. Instead of inadequacy, you imagine feeling fully capable. Rather than apprehension, you imagine feeling anticipation. Rather than frustration, you imagine feeling contentment.

3. Use your imagination to answer this question: "If I felt _____ (the opposite of my negative emotion), what action would I take in this situation?" List all of your options.

As an example, let's take these simple steps in the area of forgiveness. Imagine you've been betrayed by someone close to you. Anger, bitterness, resentment, hurt, and disappointment are boiling inside you. You recognize that despite the person's wrongdoing—and lack of an apology—you must forgive. "For if you forgive men their trespasses, your heavenly Father will also forgive you. But if you do not forgive men their trespasses, neither will your Father forgive your trespasses," Matthew 6:14-15 tells us.

Forgiveness is necessary for your own healing, and it frees you from the negative emotions that can stunt your spiritual and personal growth and even your creativity. Once you acknowledge your negative emotions, imagine feeling the opposite toward the person who betrayed you. Imagine sending the person love and mercy. Imagine that the hurtful action was born of this person's own stunted spiritual and personal growth and caused by the same negative emotions you have been feeling. Then ask yourself, If I felt love, mercy, and forgiveness toward this person, what action would I take? Your exploration list might look something like this:

- I would forgive him or her.
- I would pray for him or her.
- I would ask myself, What can I learn from this situation?
- I would free myself from focusing my time and energy on negativity about this person.
- I would ask myself, What steps do I need to take to recover from this betrayal and move forward?
- I would not allow negative emotions to spill over into other relationships and situations, molding me into an angry, bitter person.

What possibilities can you explore in your spiritual life? Perhaps it is time for a change—becoming involved in a new church ministry, spending daily time alone with God, or reading His Word each morning. Just try it and see how it feels to do something new spiritually.

What possibilities can you explore in your finances? Is financial freedom a possibility? Of course it is. But it will require you to explore your options and consider taking actions you have never considered before. Let your imagination run free. Then explore how you can get from here to there.

You must have the courage to start somewhere, even if you are uncertain where your exploration will lead. The fear of discovering that your talent isn't as strong as you think it is can paralyze you. The fear that your idea is silly can keep you stuck. The fear that you'll "do it wrong" can keep you from getting started. You can overcome these fears by moving forward anyway. That's what courage is all about: moving forward in the face of fear. With each step your fears and doubts will begin to fade. And you'll soon realize that there was nothing to fear in the first place.

As one thing leads to another, you see layers of possibilities. When you explore, you discover the vastness of your potential. This allows you to begin thinking about the ways in which you can maximize your many talents, gifts, and desires. You can then paint a picture of how your spiritual, financial, professional, and personal life all fit together to enable you to continually bring forth creativity.

❧ WALKING YOUR PATH ❧

Listen to Your Life: Tap into Your Creativity

Place a check mark in front of every statement that is true for you.

____ I am open to doing things differently just to try something new.

____ When encountering people who are different from me, I am interested in learning more about them.

____ The idea of blazing a trail is exciting to me.

____ I have created my own opportunities in the past when it was the only way for me to reach a goal.

____ I am excited about creating my own opportunities in the future.

____ Fear is not an issue for me and doesn't keep me from moving forward.

____ Creativity is a process that I enjoy very much.

____ I always explore many options before making a decision.

____ I am full of creative ideas.

____ My creativity has resulted in positive, productive opportunities.

____ Although I relate well to people, I do not always "fit in" with the crowd.

____ I am an open vessel through which God brings to life ideas, projects, and creations of all types.

If you could not answer yes to these questions, begin exploring ways to tap into your creativity so that God can use you in an even greater way.

5-Minute Action Step

For the next five minutes, think creatively and picture yourself succeeding at a level much greater than you have previously achieved. Imagine what you look like, the circumstances surrounding you, the people who are impacted in a positive way, and how it feels to succeed at that level. Incorporate this type of creative visualization into your daily routine—before you go to bed or when you first awaken.

48-Hour Challenge

In the next two days, I challenge you to get your creative juices flowing. Take time (at least an hour) to fully immerse yourself in an environment that takes you away from your normal routine. Perhaps you will spend time in an outdoor setting, visit a museum, take a ride in the country, or follow a new route home from work. You may even decide to go away for a weekend—away from all the chores and projects that normally consume your attention. While you are in your new environment or immediately after you return, revisit your vision. If your current approach doesn't seem to be moving you toward making your vision a reality, identify three alternative options for accomplishing your vision.

✦ PRAYER OF CREATIVITY ✦

Help me tap into the creativity that exists within me. Free me of the need to always do things the way they have been done and instead open my mind to new possibilities. I do not want to bury my potential by refusing to fully use all of the talents and gifts You have placed within me. As Your child, I understand that I was created in Your image, and as the Creator of the universe, You are the most creative being the world has ever seen. Therefore, creativity is my birthright as Your child. Help me claim that birthright. Remove any blocks that keep my creative juices from flowing. Enable me to see old situations in a new light. Give me the courage to create opportunities where none previously existed, and release any fear that would prevent me from doing so. Thank you for the perfect example of creativity that You have set. I pray that I will always listen to my life so that my creativity can be unleashed and You can use me as a vessel for Your purpose and Your will. Amen.

EXPECTANCY

Living in a Way that Attracts Success

If you think you can, you can.
And if you think you can't, you're right.
—MARY KAY ASH, cosmetics pioneer

When you are expecting visitors, you prepare for their arrival, right? For example, if your aunt and uncle accept an invitation to stay in your home for a week, you prepare the guest room and go shopping for extra groceries. You may arrange to take some time off from work so you can accompany them on some fun outings or perhaps sightseeing. You tell your friends, "I have family coming in this Friday. I'd love for you to stop by and meet them." Whatever form your welcome may take, I would guess you won't wait for your guests to show up before you begin to prepare. And if they don't arrive when expected, you might make some calls to check on their well-being, to be sure nothing has happened to prevent their visit.

On the other hand, if you didn't really believe they would show up, you wouldn't make the necessary preparations. You might not even be home when they arrive. Even if you were home, they would likely be surprised, perhaps disappointed, by your lack of preparation. They might decide to stay elsewhere so they wouldn't inconvenience you, which would confirm your doubts about their visit. In the end, you would both be disappointed about missing out on an opportunity to connect and enjoy a good visit.

In a similar way, people often say they expect success, but their behavior doesn't support their statement. They connect with God, with others, and with themselves, and they discover a personal mission for which they are passionate. They address the challenges that could hold them back and create a compelling vision and imaginative ideas for achieving it—but then they stop. Their purpose fits them and the vision excites them, but they do not truly expect success on the level they've dreamed of, so they don't keep moving forward in tangible ways. Then, when success doesn't come, they are devastated, disappointed, and permanently discouraged. But the fact is, if they truly expected success, they would continue to persevere until they got exactly what they were expecting. Any less-than-ideal results for their efforts would be viewed as nothing more than lessons on their journey.

Anyone who truly wants to experience life at his or her highest potential must practice the principle of expectancy: behaving, communicating, preparing, and persevering in ways that demonstrate the confidence that specific actions will lead to success. Expectancy allows you to continue walking when the exhaustion of the journey leaves you ready to give up. When you believe you are on the right path but have yet to see your vision come to fruition, expectancy washes away the doubt and calls forth the faith to keep going.

WHAT ARE YOU EXPECTING?

As we discussed in the previous chapter, everything in life begins with a thought, which is why it is imperative to listen to your thoughts and notice their impact on your life. "For as [a person] thinks in his heart, so is he," Proverbs 23:7 proclaims. The life you are now living began in your mind. Years ago particular thoughts led to particular actions—and those actions set the stage for your current reality. Now, as you look toward a future of true success, you can deliberately choose to allow an attitude of positive expectancy to permeate your thoughts, leading to actions that will result in what you expect and want most.

But you must first answer this question: What am I *expecting?*

What are you expecting in your life right now? Are you expecting good things to come your way? Or are you expecting struggle and turmoil? Do you expect that you can have the love you want? Whatever you are truly expecting, it is likely you'll get it.

In every area of your life—career, relationships, finances, spiritual life, and physical and emotional health—your actions are based upon your expectations of success or failure. A person who expects to succeed will do the things that fall in line with success. A person expecting failure will hesitate and allow fear to keep him or her from moving forward. In essence, those who expect good things to come to them will exhibit behaviors that attract success and repel those things that do not serve their lives in meaningful ways. Often, we don't even recognize when we are expecting failure.

Take a moment and compare what you say with what you actually do. As we all know, actions speak louder than words. Look into the various areas of your life, particularly the areas where you are struggling, stagnant, or frustrated, and ask yourself the following questions:

1. What am I expecting?

2. What specific actions am I currently taking that support this expectation?

For example, if you are expecting your business or career to take off, the actions aligned with that expectation would include seeking opportunities for growth, making connections with people who will help bring that expectation to life, dressing for success, and marketing your skills assertively and creatively. But if you focus on the negatives of your current circumstances rather than possibilities for the future, your actions indicate that you are expecting failure, not success. By the same token, if your relationships are filled with worry and doubt that keep you from expressing your truest self and the love you have to offer, it is likely you are expecting failure, not success. You create a self-fulfilling prophecy, and the resulting failure reinforces your negative expectation.

My challenge to you is this: Start *expecting* your path to unfold in an extraordinary way. Expect the relationship of your dreams. Expect the opportunity to advance in your career. Expect money to flow into your path. Expect to be and look healthy. Expect people to treat you with respect. Expect to have fun. Expect success! Then behave and talk as though you believe it will come.

You have the power to create what you want in your life by expecting more and taking action, one day at a time.

My friend Donna Richardson Joyner epitomizes positive expectancy. An author and wellness expert, Donna has starred in more than twenty award-winning fitness videos as well as on ESPN's *Fitness Pros* and *Crunch Fitness*. She has also served as the fitness expert for NBC's *Weekend Today* show for six years. And she was the first woman for whom Nike created a shoe, the Air Max Mundo, an aerobics training shoe.

Just how did she do all that? Throughout her career and life, Donna has aligned her actions with positive expectations. She began as a fitness instructor making $3.25 an hour and was later promoted to health club director before losing her job when the club closed down. After this happened, Donna dreamed even bigger and began hosting her own workouts. Eventually she had a stable of fifty instructors teaching classes. Then she raised the bar again and began competing in fitness competitions around the world, catching the eye of ESPN executives. At each step along the way, she expected great things to happen and aligned her actions with those expectations.

After making so many videos produced by other companies, Donna came up with an idea for a trio of videos that would help people have fun while getting in shape. I watched as she moved from talking about what she wanted to do and began taking action to do it. Not content to allow anyone to tamper with her creativity, she decided to produce the project herself. She believed in it, and with her enthusiasm and a great idea, she was able to get a lot of other people to believe in it as well. She expected it to succeed and took action based on that expectation. The videos have sold in the thousands to enthusiastic audiences wanting to become healthier.

Within a few months, opportunities began to open in a whole new arena—ministering to Christians about taking care of their bodies, temples of the Holy Spirit. A new ministry, Sweating in the Spirit, was born, along with a new television show, numerous engagements, and the chance to reach a new segment of the population with a godly message.

What Your Life Is Saying About Expectancy

How do you know when you need to enhance your level of expectancy?
- You are ready to give up, even though you have not received divine guidance to turn in a new direction.
- Your faith is waning.
- You are not actively preparing for the next destination on your path.
- You don't expect success.
- You are not fully committed to following your unique path.
- You are not confident in your skills, abilities, and vision.
- Your expectations are low.

How do you know when you are truly expecting success?
- You are willing to make major changes in your life if those changes will move you toward your vision.
- You prepare for action even when you see no evidence that opportunities are just around the corner.
- You take consistent action toward your goals.
- You anticipate growth and opportunities.
- You love what you do for a living!
- You view success as fun and attainable if you take the right steps on the right path.
- You consider yourself blessed and highly favored.

Donna's story reveals how living with an expectancy of success and aligning your actions with that expectation can lead to achieving your highest potential. In the pages ahead, we'll examine some practical ways to put the power of expectancy to work in your life.

Expectancy Multiplies Your
Opportunities for Success

If you are familiar with investment principles, then you are probably aware of the concept of compound interest, which allows your money to grow at an astounding rate when you consistently invest over a period of time. Picture yourself walking a path on which, at each successive milestone, you double your financial reward. At the first milestone you reap twenty-five cents. You have taken baby steps, and you are making progress. At the next milestone, you receive fifty cents. At the third milestone, one dollar awaits you. By the eighth milestone, you still want to reach the vision, but you're exhausted. You're weary of scaling the obstacles in your path, and quite frankly, you feel the rewards you're reaping don't match the effort you're putting forth. On the eighth milestone, you reap thirty-two dollars, but the terrain is rugged and rain is pouring down. It's hard to see your vision from this vantage point, and you're blinded to how much progress you've made. Your financial reward already is 128 times its size at the first milestone. The compounding investment of focus and consistent action is beginning to pay off, but it simply feels as though nothing significant will ever happen.

Let's say you have the faith and wisdom to stay on the path even though your vision seems unattainable and your mind becomes clouded with doubt. Occasionally you may be knocked back a few steps, or even knocked down. Your pace may slow, but if you just keep moving forward, your persistence will pay off. Eight milestones later at step sixteen, your reward grows to $8,192. And eight steps after that? The reward has grown to $2,097,152.

I use a financial example not to suggest that you are on your path to reap material rewards, but to illustrate the value of persistence. There is a "tipping point" on your path when your progress expands by leaps and bounds. (Author Malcolm Gladwell described this phenomenon in detail in his book *The Tipping Point: How Little Things Can Make a Big Difference*.) The secret is to continue walking along your path with anticipation of what you believe you will see, even when success is slow in coming. As you practice the principle of expectancy, you live in a way that empowers you to consistently attract opportunities into your path that will build upon one another, compounding your investment over time.

When you study the lives of some of the world's most successful people, you'll find that perseverance and persistence are two of the traits they commonly share. They expect success and they get it—eventually. In fact, in the early steps of their journey, they may experience more failure than success. However, a strong sense of destiny and vision keeps them focused and persistent despite any obstacles or failures along the way. What they expect is success. And they know that if they hang in there long enough, they'll get exactly what they expect.

And so will you.

Cultivating the attitude that you have every right to be wildly successful in fulfilling your mission in life will serve to make you a success magnet. You'll notice that opportunities to try new and exciting things present themselves on a regular basis. People may call you "lucky." (You know it's much more than just *luck,* but from what they can tell, you've got the Midas touch.)

Brigadier General Velma Richardson epitomizes an attitude of expectancy. By connecting with an inner knowing that a career in the U.S. Army was her calling and using as a role model her aunt who achieved the rank of colonel, she determined to become an officer. "People believe successful people are lucky," she told me when I asked her about her path to success. "But actually, you make opportunities by your actions and you open your own doors." Today, General Richardson is the highest ranking African American woman in the U.S. Army, and one of just a dozen women who currently hold the rank of general.

"I listen for God's messages, and I consistently receive confirmation from God when I am on the right path," she says. This woman of vision has concluded that being passionate and expecting success involves deliberate decisions.

Let's explore some of the actions that reflect an attitude of expectancy and help you attract the success you expect.

Move Forward in Confidence

One of the ironies of success is that it tends to elude those who struggle most in pursuing it, while the most successful people generally struggle very little, if at all. I don't mean they aren't working to succeed, but their actions are born out of a sense of purpose, not desperation. At first glimpse this seems almost cruel. Why would the highest levels of success be found by those who don't struggle as much to attain it? I believe the answer is that some people have an attitude of positive expectancy that attracts success. Since positive expectancy comes from a God-inspired mission and vision rather than a set of ego-driven goals, those individuals don't feel the need to struggle; they just boldly walk forward on their own unique path.

When I began coaching Richard, he was intent on building a business from the ground up. But he was not able to attract the right kind of clients. As a result, he spent a great deal of time on projects he did not really want, accepting fees that were lower than he deserved. He talked a good game, but his confidence level did not match his abilities, which was reflected by his posture and his timidity in asking for new business. He was prepared educationally to do the work but was not prepared entrepreneurially to generate business and market himself successfully. He was more in love with the *idea* of being successful than with doing the work it takes to *be* successful. Rather than laying the groundwork, setting up systems, and making the right contacts, he buried himself in the planning process.

My intuition told me that Richard was on the wrong path—pursuing a vision based on ego rather than purpose. But as I gently questioned him about his true desires and motives, he resisted the invitation to explore other options and continued busily pursuing success. He was always rushing from one appointment to another, yet he seemed to be spinning his wheels. He would revamp his plan and send it to me with an outline of action items. Then when we met for our sessions, he could identify only a few, if any, actions he had actually taken to move forward on the plan. The plan was workable, strategic, and creative, but the most brilliant plan is of no consequence if you don't act on it.

"You have a terrific plan, Richard, but you haven't taken action," I said during one coaching session. "What is keeping you from following through?"

He responded that as much as he hated to admit it, he didn't really believe he could pull it off. He was intimidated by the people he needed to connect with and did not expect to win their business. Despite this belief, he pretended he was pursuing a plan when he was really just playing around with it, exhausting and frustrating himself in the process.

Richard's attitude and actions stand in sharp contrast to the woman who truly believes she is capable of building a multimillion-dollar company. She will be bold enough to lay the groundwork, gain the experience, make the contacts, and act on her plan. She will expect to have the opportunity to propose high-dollar projects to prospective clients and win those clients over. Because she expects to attract the right kind of success, she exudes confidence, trusts her instincts, expands her base of knowledge on a daily basis, and looks the part of a successful entrepreneur. She expects only those who share her vision and values to work for her. Not surprisingly, top-quality employees are drawn to her company. Together, she and her team attract the right clients. The excellent work they do brings more business their way. This demonstrates not only positive expectancy but her mastery of connection. With a clear sense of purpose and self, she has the confidence to connect with others who share her vision and business values.

When you fully believe that you will be successful, those around you will begin to believe it too. Their belief in you will have a reciprocal effect, giving you more confidence as you take steps on your path. This sense of confidence will lead you to make bold moves, take bigger risks, and live more fearlessly than ever before. In reality, the moves and risks will appear bolder to others than they do to you. When you believe in the destiny that will be brought forth through the fulfillment of your highest potential, making decisions that support your vision doesn't seem bold and risky.

Of course, it is always crucial to note the difference between confidence and cockiness. Confidence is your firm belief in your abilities, talents, knowledge, or skills. Cockiness reflects an attitude that says that because of your abilities, talents, knowledge, or skills (perceived or real), you are somehow better than others who do not possess the same. Cockiness is rooted in personal insecurities and can actually weaken your ability to attract success. Confidence, on the other hand, is based upon being secure in who you are and knowing where you're headed.

Confidence will attract what you desire into your path and help you understand that things do not have to go as you planned them for you to still find success. Once you begin to exercise your faith by believing completely in your purpose, you operate your life with a solid belief that things will work out the way they should. You have confidence that whatever happens is meant to happen, and you have an unfailing belief that God will ensure that all things in your life will in some way work together for good. God wants to know that we trust His timing, His purpose, and His ways. By doing this, we attract divine favor and grace to fulfill our highest potential.

Go Where You Expect to Find Success

When you are living your mission, opportunities flow naturally into your path because you are where you are supposed to be, living the life you were meant to live. In essence, just by walking your unique path, you attract success.

By walking your path, you are doing the work you were created to do. I'm not talking about work only in a career sense, but work in the sense of your mission in life. When you use your natural gifts and talents to make a positive impact on the world, you are doing your work, whether it is solving a dispute or singing in the choir or creating jobs through your company or sharing your love with those who need it or writing a book that inspires others. Whatever constitutes the work you were sent here to do, doing your work means taking steps on your path.

As you take those steps, you attract more of the blessings and opportunities you want in your life. If you chose instead to walk another path, the blessings and opportunities would still be on your path, but you would not be there to experience them. They would go to someone else, wither away, or simply wait for you to eventually show up.

For example, if your goal is to be a television producer, then turning down an offer out of college to work as a receptionist at a local network affiliate to take a better-paying job as a marketing specialist for a health-care company may be a decision you regret for years to come. Why? Because the lower-paying job may well put you in the right environment to meet the right people who will provide opportunities that would eventually lead to producing. If you are willing to accept a smaller income for a year to work in the receptionist job, you may find that in four months you are a production assistant, and in another year you are an associate producer—and you continue to move up from there. The key is taking the risk and making the "sacrifice" to be in the right place.

Several years ago a friend of mine who wanted very much to work in the entertainment public relations arena made a bold move. Although she was already working in public relations for a major performing arts entity in Dallas, she wanted a taste of the "big time." She ventured to New York a couple of times for interviews. Several companies expressed interest, but she seemed to keep losing out to local people who could start right away and didn't need a relocation package. When her roommate became engaged and decided to move the following month, she began reevaluating her situation. Then it hit her out of the blue. "I'll move to New York!"

When she called me, she sounded worried that I might think she had gone crazy. After all, she didn't have a job lined up there, and admittedly she did not have much in savings. But I was thoroughly excited about her decision. "That's fantastic!" I told her. "It takes a lot of guts, but I believe you're going to do just great in New York. It's what you want. Even if you have to wait tables for a couple of months until you get the job you want, it will be worth it."

With a handful of contacts and an attitude of expectancy, she packed up and moved. A few weeks later, she was interviewing with some of the biggest entertainment and media companies in the world, and she landed a job she loved. She was in the right place when opportunity intersected her path.

SET BOUNDARIES TO PROTECT YOUR SPACE

Many distractions can interfere with your ability to attract success into your life, which is why it's crucial to set boundaries to protect your space.

Your "space" is your "personal magnetic field" that attracts success. Your space can become cluttered with things that serve no real purpose for you and interfere with your ability to attract what you would truly like to have in your life.

In other words, too much extraneous stuff will weaken your magnetic field. So in order to attract your highest level of success, you must be serious about protecting this important space. For some people, this comes easily. For others, especially people pleasers, it can be a bit more difficult. I fit into the latter category, but after consistent practice, I've finally learned to protect my space. I still haven't mastered it, but I've made major progress!

Here are some key strategies for protecting your space:

- Be clear—to yourself and others—about what you want in your space.
- Be clear about what you don't want.
- Be willing to say no to offers and opportunities you don't want.
- Embrace the idea that you have the right to say yes or no to any question. Just because someone else feels you should do something, doesn't mean you have to agree. In order to follow your divinely ordained path, you must have room in your schedule to do what needs to be done.
- Recognize that by saying yes to something you don't really want, you may in essence be saying no to something you really do want. This is particularly true if the thing you say yes to leaves you less time to spend on what you want.

As you read through that list, did you struggle with the idea of telling someone no? Fear of saying no can cause a great deal of stress. It's the source of countless lies: "Oh, I really appreciate your invitation, but I have to work late that night." "I would let you borrow my car, but…uh…I'm getting a tune-up that day." or "Will I fill in for John while he's on vacation? Sure, I'd love to." Of course, once you tell a lie, you hold firmly to it or else risk being discovered, thereby adding more stress to your life.

I am convinced that the world would be a healthier, happier place if more people became comfortable with using that little two-letter word *no*. More people would spend their time doing what they really want to be doing. Fewer people would be inclined to please everyone else and would embark on a journey of being true to themselves and God.

I suggest this simple rule: If your answer is not a definite yes, then say no. This rule will enrich your life in more ways than you might think, and it will save you headaches and stress. Remember to listen to your life when someone asks you to take on a new task or invest your time and emotional energy in something. Follow your intuition. It is divine guidance that directs you on your path. If your intuition says no, let your mouth do the same.

You have the right to say no to requests that fall outside your purpose and vision or infringe upon your boundaries. Remember, you are working to align your actions with your expectations, not someone else's. If your vision is to live a life of more peace and less stress, and you've scheduled a day to do absolutely nothing, then honor your decision. Refuse to get sucked back into your work or the agenda of others. Of course, there are exceptions and emergencies, but barring those, honor your plans. Don't feel that you must give a long explanation when you decline an invitation. A simple "I have plans" will suffice.

There is an art to saying no gracefully. The secret is to be straight-forward yet helpful. For example, if a friend asks you to baby-sit and you feel like resting, tell the truth and suggest an alternative: "I'm exhausted, so it's just not going to be a good day for me to baby-sit. Have you considered asking Janet's daughter? She's sixteen and baby-sits all the time. She's great with children." With this response, you can say no gracefully and focus the conversation on a possible solution.

Telling the truth and saying no without apologies is empowering. It is a sign of personal growth and of your ability to stand up for what you want. It allows you to take control of how your time is spent, and it frees you to say yes to the things that matter most.

CULTIVATING AN IMAGE OF SUCCESS

A vital component of expecting success is looking the part. Whatever you are seeking to attract, ask yourself, Do I look like someone who could attract *that* into my life? Sadly, I have seen success elude many talented people because they did not understand the importance of their image. I also have seen success attach to people who lack exceptional talent but who understand the value of an effective and powerful image.

No single look attracts success. Like everything else we have discussed in this book, your successful look is unique to you. It is based on what you do, what you seek, and who you are. Your look should be a celebration of those elements of yourself that are most important. Obviously, if your passion and talents lie in the area of finance and you seek to attract success on Wall Street, mimicking the style that has attracted success to, let's say, Madonna probably will not be a wise strategy for you. On the flip side, if your passion and talents lead you to a vision of being a makeup artist to the stars, inspiration from style makers in the celebrity world may be just what you need to attract the right opportunities.

When you look the part of what you want, others tend to see your potential and begin to treat you as though the success you desire is already yours. Here are some steps you can take to look the part of someone who expects to attract success:

- Consider the look of those who are successful in the ways you aim to be successful. How do they enhance their attributes?

- Honestly evaluate yourself. Most likely that means seeking input from those whose style you admire or seeking a professional evaluation from an image consultant.
- Be willing to make changes. You don't have to do everything at once, but you must be willing to do *something*, unless your look is already working for you.
- Make sure your fashion style matches your personal and career style.
- Make sure your hairstyle celebrates your personality and style.
- Consider your posture and stance. Do you walk with confidence? Remember, confidence is attractive.
- Do you dislike anything about your appearance? If so, what steps can you take to improve it? Make a plan and take action! From a more fit body to whiter teeth, you have the power to be more attractive simply by deciding to.
- Smile more! One of the easiest ways to become more attractive is to greet people in a way that makes them feel welcome. When people feel welcomed and appreciated, they are more likely to do things that will keep you smiling.

It's Time to Wake Up!

When I was a little girl, I had a Bugs Bunny alarm clock on my dresser. Bugs was my favorite cartoon character, mainly because he always outsmarted the Road Runner, and I was delighted to wake up to the sound of him announcing, "Uhhh… Wake up, doc!" My mother still marvels at how I would sit straight up in bed, stretch out my arms, and smile as I awakened from a deep sleep. "Good morning!" I would greet her as she walked into the room.

"I've never seen anybody wake up happy like that every single day," she'd say. At that age, I was always excited at the prospect of a new day. Life was fun, hassle-free, and somewhat of an adventure. I felt prepared to face each day and conquer any challenges that might come my way. I expected good things!

Although I would not have used the word *potential* then, it was the potential that each new day offered that prompted me to wake up happy and excited. After all, my mother had prepared me well by teaching me to read and write before I entered kindergarten. So, heading off to school, I was confident and eager to learn more. Besides school, I looked forward to gymnastics classes and playing with the many friends who lived on my street. And if they were busy, there was always my sandbox and swing set in the backyard—I could be quite content playing alone.

In that environment, I excelled. Why? Because I was prepared, confident, supported, and optimistic. Most important, I lived each day in the moment. This skill is perhaps most easily mastered by children, but it can be reclaimed by adults.

The process of waking up is a great analogy for living in the moment. Most people who have difficulty waking up in the morning dread the present moment. They would rather stick with the safety and unconsciousness of the nighttime hours, so they procrastinate when the moment arrives for them to wake up. But sleeping when it's time to wake up is never enjoyable sleep because the cloud of knowing you should be up hovers low. The same holds true when you decide to hit the snooze button in your life. The potential exists to do something today that could positively change your life, but the choice to wake up and do it is yours.

Your potential is not a destination you reach, but rather an unlimited possibility that something greater is available if you will open yourself to it. You have to expect something! Moving toward your potential is a process of growth that signals you are alive.

Think about it. If you are not growing, you are spiritually dead. For every living organism on earth, the evidence of its life is growth, movement, and change. You may not grow any taller, but parts of your physical being are constantly growing and changing—your hair, nail, and skin cells perpetually reproduce. Your shape changes. Your heart beats. Your lungs breathe. Your body moves. It is evidence of life! In the same way, your spiritual being is in a constant state of growth—learning, improving, and changing. When that happens, the capacity of your potential grows with you. That is why you can look back over your life and see things that come easily today but were difficult in the past.

If you are alive, you are growing. You are moving toward something more in your life. You are becoming a healthier, more peaceful, loving, and successful person. In contrast, when you are spiritually dead, there is nothing new in your life—no new ideas, no new growth, no new opportunities. If we are honest with ourselves, we have all had dead moments in our lives—times when we have felt stuck, confused, or depressed. This may be the place you find yourself in right now. You don't feel like doing anything, so you don't. You want a new job, but you never take action to bring that desire to life. You are sick of a relationship, but you do nothing to change or end it. You have an idea, but you never move on it. You want more, but you never expect more.

This world is full of the walking dead. They are around us every day, and quite frankly, they are not particularly fond of those of us who are truly living. We are proof of their deadness.

Perhaps you're not dead, but you are staying in bed as long as possible, trying to get those last few minutes of "sleep." You're moving but dragging your feet along the way. Your spirit wants you to raise your expectations, but you are fighting it.

The only hurdle to waking up—or resurrecting your passion—and taking control of your life is making a decision to do so. You can decide today to live in the expectation of success. What treasures are lying dormant in your life? What dream do you need to awaken? What relationship needs new life? As you identify the possibilities on your path, your senses will awaken. Your vision will help you tap into positive expectancy in your life. You don't have to see all of the possibilities, but if you can just get a glimpse, it will be enough to wake you up and get you moving.

So practice dreaming while you are awake. Imagine the possibilities for your life. Allow yourself to get excited about them. Don't cover them up, bury them, or allow them to lie dormant. It's time to wake up! You can create positive expectancy in your life by simply taking steps on your path. But taking steps requires you to get up and get moving!

⚜ WALKING YOUR PATH ⚜

Listen to Your Life: What Are You Expecting?

Place a check mark in front of every statement that is true for you.

___ My actions during the last week have indicated my absolute belief that God will do exceedingly abundantly above all I can ever ask or think (Ephesians 3:20).

___ I consistently take action to bring my vision to fruition.

___ My positive outlook on life often rubs off on those around me.

___ Opportunities seem to flow easily into my path.

___ Being successful is fun for me.

___ I believe that I can succeed well beyond my current level.

___ In every area of my life (finances, relationships, health and fitness, etc.), I feel that I will have what I want most in God's timing.

___ If an opportunity presented itself today for me to fulfill my greatest desire, I would be ready to take advantage of it.

___ I never miss an opportunity to move further along my path.

___ The faith I profess is clearly reflected in the way I live my life.

If any of the above statements were not true for you, it is important to actively counter the negative thinking that plagues you with the truth of God's Word.

5-Minute Action Step

Take a close look at yourself today. Do you look like someone who can accomplish your compelling vision? Are your actions and choices in line with where you say you are headed? List five specific ways in which you could enhance your image and align your actions with your vision.

1.

2.

3.

4.

5.

48-Hour Challenge

One of the keys to creating an attitude of positive expectancy is imprinting the promises of God's Word on your spirit. You must know, without a doubt, what God says about you, your purpose, and your potential. Not only does this help you maintain the right mind-set, but when negative thoughts enter your mind, you can counter them with God's truth. In the next forty-eight hours, identify at least five verses from the Bible that speak to your needs and will help you walk fearlessly on the path that God has for you.

1.

2.

3.

4.

5.

❧ Prayer of Expectancy ❧

God, show me where my actions are not aligned with my dreams and enable me to live with the highest level of personal integrity. Reveal to me every area of my life where my stated expectations are not demonstrated by my actions. Your Word says that "a dream comes through much activity, but a fool's voice is known by his many words." Ecclesiastes 5:3 I don't want to be that fool who talks about my dreams and never does anything to bring them to fruition. Where I am having trouble believing the promises of Your Word, bring me into contact with people who can be examples of faith in action. Allow me not to be intimidated by them but to learn from them. Wherever negative expectancy is causing me to sabotage my own success in relationships, finances, health, spiritual growth, career, or any area that plagues me, help me break the cycle of failure. Jesus said, "Whatever...you ask in prayer, believing, you will receive." Matthew 21:22 I believe right now that You are delivering me from any negative emotion, doubt, fear, or unbelief that would keep me off my path. Open my eyes to any negative self-fulfilling prophecies that have manifested in my life, and give me the wisdom and courage to reverse them. Help me raise my expectations about what is possible in my life. Give me the courage and creativity to reach for something more, something better than I have previously known. Show me how to look and act the part of the person You are shaping me into. And help me attract success naturally using the gifts and experiences You have given me. Amen.

FLOW

Adapting to the Unexpected Twists and Turns of Life

If you faint in the day of adversity,
Your strength is small.

—PROVERBS 24:10

So often in today's world, we are taught to balance our lives. If we give equal attention to all of the right things, we're told, our lives will be healthy and fulfilling. Sounds easy enough—but how many of us actually succeed in our pursuit of balance?

The word *balance* brings to mind a performer walking on a tightrope, arms outstretched, with a dangerous fall looming if he makes the slightest wrong move. Many people can relate to this image because they're attempting to balance while carrying an immense load of all the "right" things—and feeling as though they might fall off the tightrope at any moment.

In the letters and e-mails I receive, a common question is, "How can I find balance?" One reader wrote that she was raising three children, working full time, and attending college full time. She wanted my advice on how she could find balance in her life so that she could pursue her dream of having her own business. Clearly, everything that she was doing and dreamed of doing could be considered "good." But taking on all of these things at once made her load so heavy that it threatened to leave her too fatigued to continue on her path, let alone plan for a better future. Balance was not her primary need.

If you think about it, trying to balance a load while juggling it is not the most natural thing in the world. That's why I recommend focusing less on balance—though it has its place—and relying more on the principle of "flow."

For me it helps to think of flow in the context of a river. Imagine that your path is a river with twists and turns, calm and serene points, rapids and waterfalls. If you flow with the river, you enjoy the smoothest journey. You may get bruised along the way, but not as badly as if you fought the currents and tired yourself out so that you had no energy left for your journey.

When people resist change in certain areas of their lives, it is usually because they feel they must compensate when things do not go according to plan. As a result, when heavier loads are added, they attempt to find a new "center of balance." The problem with this strategy is that it wears you out. The heavier your load, the more difficult it is to balance. Flowing, on the other hand, gives you flexibility in your life and allows you to follow the path of least resistance that has been uniquely designed for you.

Of course, there is more to flow than serving as an alternative to balance. Flow is about adjusting your priorities to cope with change, tuning in to life's natural rhythm and God's timing, finding purpose in your pain, increasing your capacity to handle more of what life brings, and enjoying the journey even when you're forced to take an unexpected detour.

Adjusting Your Priorities as You Go

By virtue of life's tendency to throw curve balls from time to time, you need to be prepared to adjust your priorities so that you will experience the best that life has to offer, even in the midst of challenging times. At various points, certain aspects of your life will require more attention than others. Without an awareness that priorities are ever-changing rather than constant, you'll find yourself struggling to deal with new responsibilities, opportunities, and issues that come into your life.

As you connect with God and yourself, you can clearly identify the current priorities in your life and begin living in a way that allows you to flow in the direction those priorities take you. This is not to say that you should neglect or ignore any area. However, you must prioritize what needs your attention most in order for your path to unfold in the best possible way. You'll recall from the chapter on vision that what we focus on will expand. We must be careful not to expand something in our lives that will block the flow of something more important.

For example, your family may need more of your time than usual right now—perhaps someone is ill or you've just welcomed a new baby or your spouse is feeling discouraged or your teenager is struggling in school. Whatever the circumstance, there are times when family becomes a greater priority than, let's say, career. Although you may not have achieved your career goals, you recognize that you cannot and do not want to deal with the consequences that may come with attempting to do and have everything. For one thing, you would suffer—with stress, exhaustion, and frustration. And your work and family would suffer, because you cannot do everything really well simultaneously. So you choose to allow a greater amount of your time than usual to flow toward strengthening your family relationships and meeting needs. The shift is not permanent, but it gives you the grace to fulfill your divine assignment at that given point in time.

I came to this realization firsthand when a sudden and near-fatal health crisis struck my family. One December evening as I was chatting on the phone with my mother about the events of the day, she experienced an

What Your Life Is Saying About Flow

How do you know if you're struggling against the flow of life?

- When turbulent waters come, your immediate response is "Why me?" rather than "What is this experience telling or teaching me?"
- Similar types of problems keep plaguing your life, but you're not seeking a way to solve them.
- The adversities of life weaken you.
- You are frustrated, angry, or bitter as a result of the trials and tribulations you have faced.
- Inconveniences such as waiting in line, being stuck in a traffic jam, or adjusting your plans for a last-minute change regularly frustrate you.

How do you know you have learned to go with the flow of life?

- You are able to handle more in your life—whether good opportunities or bad news. You have increased your capacity to deal with whatever life may send your way.
- You can remain calm when life's storms churn around you.
- In the midst of life's difficulties, you connect even more deeply with God, yourself, and others to find comfort, peace, and wisdom.
- The adversities of life strengthen you.
- You are a wiser, more faithful person as a result of the trials and tribulations you have faced.

intense and sudden pain in her head. She said she had never felt anything like it before and wanted to get off the phone so that she could take some pain reliever. Having suffered a very minor stroke earlier that year, one that had caused no physical problems, she was concerned that the pain might be something serious. She called me later to say she had spoken with two neurologists to tell them what she was feeling. Both assured her that she was not experiencing stroke symptoms and encouraged her to take some ibuprofen and lie down. I was glad to hear it.

Later that night as I sat in my home office writing a column for my newsletter, my then-eight-year-old brother called to say that our mother continued to suffer from intense pain and wanted me to come over and take her to the hospital. She thought she'd rather be safe than sorry. But even as we were talking on the phone, something in her spirit told her there simply was no time to waste—not even enough time for me to make the thirty-minute drive to pick her up. "Tell Valorie you are hanging up the phone to call 911," she said from the background, sounding violently ill.

When I arrived at the emergency room, I expected to find my mother in good condition with a diagnosis of food poisoning or something simi- lar. Instead, I found her lying on a stretcher in a deep sleep, oblivious to my touch when I squeezed her cold, limp hand. She was in a coma, and the emergency room physician was at a loss to explain what was wrong. She was rolled away for tests, which revealed that a blood vessel had burst in the cerebellum of her brain, causing a massive stroke. Before I could digest what was happening, a nurse handed me a pen to sign paperwork authorizing emergency brain surgery.

While I sat alone in the surgery waiting room, stunned and afraid of the worst, God spoke to me, and I listened: "She's going to be okay." It was a knowing in my spirit, and I never forgot it—even through a major set- back and a recovery that was slower than we hoped.

The life of each member of my family changed dramatically that evening, especially my mother's. Seven weeks later she arrived home from the hospital, blessed to be alive but unable to stand or walk. At forty-nine years old, she was struggling with impaired vision, swallowing, and speech skills, among a host of other problems.

My responsibilities shifted dramatically. I went from being a single and independent twenty-something to being responsible for my recovering mother and my eight-year-old brother. In the frightening frenzy of it all, it took a few months from the time of her stroke for me to flow with the shift in my responsibilities. I was still holding myself accountable for doing everything I had done before *plus* everything I needed to do now.

One morning as I was praying about how to continue to live my purpose in the midst of the challenging circumstances, God whispered a needed bit of wisdom to my spirit. He said, "You are still living your purpose, but I have a special assignment for you right now. I need you to be there for your mother and brother and to inspire and encourage your mother while she recovers. Keep things going professionally, but not at the same pace as before. I'll take care of everything. Don't worry." At that moment, I decided to go with the flow. I had a clear vision of my divine assignment, and I focused on fulfilling it. Our family was facing some rough waters, but I learned that going with the flow of the circumstances was much easier than resisting the inevitable.

Although I would have preferred another way of learning the wisdom I gained as a result of my mother's stroke, I am grateful for the ways in which I grew as a person as I was stretched beyond my comfort zone. The fact that my mother lived was a miracle, but that she recovered—although still challenged with a few disabilities—is an awesome testimony of God's grace and goodness. By focusing on what God was doing in her life—and mine—through this time, I was able to invest my energies in what mattered most.

SYNCHRONIZE YOUR ACTIONS
WITH GOD'S TIMING

Many people have difficulty embracing the natural rhythm of life. They expect everything to happen in their timing. They want what they want when they want it. The problem with this attitude is that we don't have a bird's-eye view to see the complete picture of life. God's perspective is always greater than ours. He sees from eternity to eternity and knows all the plans He has for us.

Consider the words of the Preacher in the book of Ecclesiastes:

To everything there is a season,
A time for every purpose under heaven:
A time to be born,
And a time to die;
A time to plant,
And a time to pluck what is planted;
A time to kill,
And a time to heal;
A time to break down,
And a time to build up;
A time to weep,
And a time to laugh;
A time to mourn,
And a time to dance;
A time to cast away stones,
And a time to gather stones;
A time to embrace,
And a time to refrain from embracing;

A time to gain,
> And a time to lose;

A time to keep,
> And a time to throw away;

A time to tear,
> And a time to sew;

A time to keep silence,
> And a time to speak;

A time to love,
> And a time to hate;

A time of war,
> And a time of peace. (3:1-8)

Clearly, there is a time for everything. Of course, it takes faith to rely on divine timing. It's not easy to go with the flow rather than trying to force our lives in a particular direction.

In what areas of life are you struggling to get in sync with divine timing?

- career
- personal finances
- love life
- entrepreneurial endeavors
- family matters
- spiritual growth
- forgiveness
- a creative endeavor

As you tune in to the divine rhythm of your life, you'll learn to wait patiently on God's timing while remaining alert to signals that it's time to move ahead.

Learning to Wait Patiently

At times we may find ourselves questioning God: *I've done all You asked me to do, Lord. Perhaps I've not done it perfectly, but I've given my best effort. I've been faithful. Why am I still waiting for my blessing?* During these times it is essential to be still and pursue your connection with God. Listen for His quiet voice telling your spirit that the time is not right—and trust Him. Often, we must wait because something better is on the way. We can't see it, but God can. Proverbs 3:5-6 says, "Trust in the LORD with all your heart, and lean not on your own understanding; in all your ways acknowledge Him, and He shall direct your paths."

Can you think of a time when you had to wait much longer than you wanted to for something, but when things finally came together, it was obvious why the timing worked out as it did? Describe what happened.

When you learn to flow naturally with life, you stop fighting the divinely orchestrated plan. You stop trying to make things happen out of season. You cease to be jealous when someone else is reaping a full harvest while you're still in the planting stage. You know your time is coming. The question is, are you willing to synchronize your timing with divine timing? Or will you insist on taking matters into your own hands, forgoing the blessings and opportunities awaiting you in exchange for instant gratification and delayed regret?

Responding When It's Time to Move Ahead

Of course, divine timing is not always about waiting. You can also disrupt the flow of your life by procrastinating. You're sitting fearfully at the edge of the water while God is telling you to jump in and swim. "I'll get in the water tomorrow," you tell yourself as life and opportunities rush by.

Procrastination is one of the most effective and consistent thieves of untapped potential. Because of it, millions of brilliant ideas never become reality. Thousands of businesses are never started. Countless books are never brought to life.

Why do so many people practice procrastination as a way of life? It offers several short-term benefits:

- You can avoid facing your fear of failure, success, rejection, and anything else that keeps you stuck.

Building on What You Know

Flow is easiest to experience when we embrace the other principles we have discussed:

1. *Connection.* Flowing takes less effort when you connect with God, yourself, and others so that you have clear wisdom and guidance for the decisions and direction you take in life. We cannot always understand why things happen, but we can trust that "there is a season, a time for every purpose under heaven" (Ecclesiastes 3:1).

2. *Self-Curiosity.* Flowing requires that you question your emotions, feelings, and actions in order to grow and overcome challenges and frustrating experiences. Without self-curiosity, you will find the adversities of life pulling you into whirlpools of despair, depression, or resentment.

3. *Vision.* Flowing is easier when you have a vision for where you are headed. When you can envision your destination, you'll be less

- It's easier to daydream about the future than to live fully in the present.
- You get to do something more enjoyable than taking a risk.
- You get to believe that you'll do it tomorrow!

But when you give in to the temptation to procrastinate, you endure plenty of negatives, such as:

- anxiety and worry about something you "should" be doing right now
- frustration about never reaching your full potential
- uneasiness about putting off an important project
- regret that you could have done a better job if you'd given yourself the time
- stress to perform under high pressure because you've waited until the last minute

inclined to give up when the journey encounters turbulence. In the Old Testament God tells the prophet Habakkuk, "Write the vision and make it plain on tablets, that he may run who reads it. For the vision is yet for an appointed time; but at the end it will speak, and it will not lie. Though it tarries, wait for it; because it will surely come, it will not tarry" (Habakkuk 2:2-3).

4. *Creativity*. Flowing is easier when you are open to creative alternatives to reaching your destination. Adversity will come. Will you see it as an obstacle or as an opportunity for exploring new ways of doing things?

5. *Expectancy*. Even in the face of adversity, you can expect that "this, too, shall pass." By exercising your faith, you continue to go with the flow because you know that something better is coming. But you will never reach it if you give up and don't keep moving on your path.

Procrastination allows you to spend your life pretending you are going to get something done while doing everything but the task at hand. As you fritter away your time with less important matters, you're filled with anxiety about the unfinished item that hangs over your head.

I have battled with procrastination most of my life. In fact, I procrastinated about writing this chapter! I have found that the best approach for me is to be completely honest with myself. If I'm not going to get a particular project done today, then I admit it. Doing so frees me to enjoy the present.

For example, rather than telling yourself that you are about to write that report—right after you clean your desk—just say, "You know what? That's not going to get done today." Then focus fully on what you *will* do. As philosopher Ralph Waldo Emerson suggested, "Finish each day and be done with it. You have done what you could; some blunders and absurdities have crept in; forget them as soon as you can."

TURBULENCE IS INEVITABLE

Not only will connecting with God help you move naturally to the rhythm of life, it will prepare you to deal with the inevitable challenges that come to all of us. If you're alert to what's happening in your life, you can brace yourself for the ride and hopefully learn something along the way.

Let's imagine that you're traveling a river in a rubber raft. You've arrived at a point where the water is calm, and you have an abundance of everything you want and need. You're tempted to jump out of the raft and take a swim in those tranquil waters. Something in your spirit tells you to stay put, but logic says you're being silly. So you plunge in. As you backstroke down the gentle river, enjoying the warm, peaceful water, you're jolted by the sudden thump of a boulder striking your head. You were swimming straight, but the river took a sharp turn that you didn't anticipate. As you shake off the blow, you look downstream and see the waters quickly turning to rapids. You need your raft! But it's ten yards downstream and gaining momentum. A major adrenaline rush propels you to swim forcefully toward the raft, and you manage to pull yourself in and brace yourself for the turbulence ahead.

If we live long enough, turbulent waters *will* come—sometimes as a result of our own bad choices and sometimes through no fault of our own. At times another person's river path crashes into ours, possibly changing the direction of our path. At other times, God sends rough waters to disrupt us when we have been sucked into an eddy of complacency or pride—or He simply wants to move us on to the next leg of the journey more quickly.

The good news is that every problem we face can birth new opportunity in our lives if we are paying attention. And fast-moving waters can serve as opportunities to expand our capacity to handle more of what life is bringing our way.

Challenges Can Birth New Purpose

If we allow them to, the turbulent floodwaters of life can lift us to higher ground—spiritually, mentally, physically, emotionally, financially, romantically, professionally, and personally. Of course, most people whose finances spiral completely out of control would rather not go bankrupt in the process of learning to better manage their finances, but often that is the end result. No one enters into marriage hoping for a divorce in order to learn how to have a more fulfilling love life, but sometimes that's what it takes for people to recognize where they've gone wrong. No one wants a heart attack to serve as a wake-up call about his or her health, but that may be the only signal that can capture a person's attention. Even when lessons come the hard way, God has a way of turning tragedy into triumph.

Difficult circumstances—whether self-inflicted or a consequence of someone else's choices—can give birth to purpose. Countless lives have been saved, tragedies avoided, and lives enriched because of people who turned their pain into something productive and meaningful. From historical figures to modern-day heroes, we can find examples from all walks of life.

Harriet Tubman, one of the most intriguing, bold, and inspiring figures in American history, exemplifies this concept. An escaped slave whose terror-filled memories of human bondage must have been etched in her mind until her dying day, she risked death to creep into the Deep South twenty-seven times to lead slaves to freedom. Her purpose was born of her pain.

When traveling and speaking, I often meet people who are changing lives in tremendous ways, using their pain and tragedy to help others. In 2000 I met Rhonda Britten, who, at fourteen years of age, experienced the unthinkable. One Sunday morning she stood in front of her house waiting for her two sisters to come out so they could all pile into the car and head out for a nice family brunch. Her father had other plans in mind. Armed with a shotgun loaded with just two bullets, he aimed and fired at her mother, killing her instantly. Then he turned the barrel squarely at Rhonda, the only witness to the incident. The thought of shooting her must have been only momentary because he instead turned the gun on himself. Rhonda watched with horror as her father killed himself.

After two decades of struggling with the emotional and mental aftermath of such a senseless and cruel tragedy, Rhonda eventually had a major breakthrough. She identified the greatest source of the issues (low self-esteem, excuses, anger) that was keeping her from fulfilling her potential: fear. She harnessed all that she had learned over the years and began sharing an inspiring message with audiences across the country. Once her speaking career began to take off, she elaborated on her message in her first book *Fearless Living*, which has helped thousands of people overcome their fears and their past. Rhonda's story is a tremendous example of refusing to live a defeated life and instead developing purpose out of pain.

While you may never have endured anything as traumatic as Rhonda, surely certain events and experiences in your life, perhaps unpleasant ones, have changed you in a profound way. Such occasions have helped shape and mold you into the person you are and have given you a unique perspective that, when used for good, can positively impact others and transform your life.

How have your pain, difficulties, and challenges contributed to your life purpose and the path you are now destined to walk?

When your path takes unexpected twists and turns and you get cut by jagged rocks and sharp debris, the best thing to do is go with the flow. Look for the lessons to be learned and use the power of expectancy to give you a vision for better days ahead. God will give you the strength you need to get through and will make you stronger in faith. Your connection with Him ensures it. Listen as that divine voice whispers comfort and wisdom to you, giving you the strength to flow with adversity and grow from the experience.

Challenges Expand Your Potential

Accepting that everything in life happens for a reason frees you to learn from your experiences. As you learn you grow, and as you grow you expand your capacity for handling more of what life holds. Remember, floods only occur when there is too much water for the river channel. If you've been stretched by experience, you have more capacity to handle the blessings that flow into your path. On the other hand, if you do not have the capacity to handle more blessings, you may find yourself drowning in opportunities and putting them all in jeopardy as a result.

For example, when Jonathan, a talented and hard-working information technology specialist, came to me, he was attracting more clients to his new consulting business than he could handle effectively. Overwhelmed by the number of clients and the intensity of the projects, he was beginning to fall behind in meeting deadlines and keeping promises he'd made to his clients. He had not put any structure in place to handle growth. Now he was experiencing a flood, and he was on the verge of drowning. Having never before been in business for himself, he simply was not ready for the challenge.

The first step for him was to prioritize his projects, and then contact clients to give them realistic completion dates. The next step was to expand his capacity by connecting with another consultant whom he could trust to work with him on the projects. By doing so, he expanded his capacity for serving more clients *and* generating more revenue. The next step was to establish a support system for handling time-consuming aspects of his business that were not the best use of his energy and skills. He contracted with a bookkeeper for a small monthly fee and made use of a virtual assistant who kept track of his schedule and returned calls and e-mails when he was out of the office. With the extra support in place, Jonathan was freed to do what he does best.

By acknowledging problems and seeking solutions, you can expand your capacity to experience higher levels of success. If you learn to view difficulties as opportunities for growth, you won't feel compelled to struggle or give up. Instead, you'll appreciate each new challenge as an adventure that can move you closer to fulfilling your vision.

LIGHTEN UP AND ENJOY YOUR PATH

Rather than flowing with life and viewing challenges as opportunities to grow and learn, many people act as if every single day is a new battle to be fought. I'm not referring to people with life-or-death problems. I'm talking about those who approach routine, everyday experiences—such as driving to work or ordering food in a restaurant—as if every action will have grave consequences.

Have you ever witnessed the anguish some people put themselves through when deciding what to order from a menu or which movie to see? Others agonize over deadlines at work or how to handle a home-improvement project.

Whenever you find yourself taking something too seriously, pause a moment to gain some perspective. It's time to lighten up. Life is too short and too precious to be weighed down with worry and self-imposed pressure.

Lightening up isn't about scheduling some downtime from the seriousness of life. It's about replacing an overly serious attitude with a lighter outlook. This is not to say that you don't take important things seriously. However, you don't need to treat every experience as though your life depends on it. That serious attitude can drain the joy out of life and prompt you to miss moments of inspiration and awe.

Often a too-serious attitude is a sign that you have assigned more value to an experience than it is worth. Perhaps you value a certain position or relationship more for its perceived ability to elevate your status than for its ability to serve your purpose or bring you joy. When you find yourself unable to keep from attaching too much weight to an experience, it is time to do some soul-searching to uncover the reasons. What does the experience symbolize for you? What need will be met by the experience? Is your attitude about it enhancing your well-being or detracting from it?

Hold Your Dreams Loosely

Often the best way to lighten up is to stop attaching so much weight to your desires and experiences. It is this weight that keeps you from being able to live a life that feels effortless. Desiring something without being attached to it requires a delicate balance. It requires wanting something, yet being willing to let it go. It involves recognizing the significance of something without allowing its presence in your life to consume you.

What do you need to be willing to let go of? Is it a relationship you desperately want? a job you think you need? a lifestyle you aspire to?

When you hold your dreams loosely, you trust God to replace them with something even better if He chooses. You know deep within your spirit that God is working all things together for His good purposes. If a desired experience doesn't come to pass, perhaps it wasn't meant to be. Don't mourn so long that you miss out on a better experience. So you didn't get the client/job/grade you wanted? It's not the end of the world. Learn from the experience and move on. It's quite likely that something better is on the way. So you thought he was "the one," but it didn't work out? Good! Now you have space in your life for the *real* one to show up.

This attitude takes faith and trust that even when you don't know the big picture of your life, God does. When we can remind ourselves that something better is coming, we become content to accept each experience for what it's worth: learning and growth. Then we are free to lighten up about the things that come our way.

For example, if your job is in jeopardy, it's quite likely that you will want to save it—unless, of course, you've been dreaming of leaving! Lightening up in this situation means putting things in perspective. Losing your job may involve adjustments or frustrations, but it will not be the end of the world. Rather than seeing this potential loss as a huge weight that will sink your career, ask yourself what opportunity it presents—perhaps a job that better suits your natural gifts and talents or a much-needed break or an opportunity to redefine your role in the organization? If you keep in mind the truth that everything in life happens for a reason, you can trust that in hindsight this perceived obstacle may in fact be a major blessing.

Enjoy the Sights Along the Way

So often we put intense pressure on ourselves to perform, to make things happen that will propel us on our path toward success. As a result, each decision or issue we face becomes a major concern rather than a new opportunity. This was a recurring theme in my own life that I finally decided to address when it was brought to my attention.

Compelled by my purpose of inspiring people to live more fulfilling, less stressful lives, I had begun to focus too much on the accomplishments I thought were necessary to reach my potential. For a long time I did not factor the influence of my words into my definition of success. Instead, a constant need to do more, to accomplish *something*, was causing me to mentally berate myself. When opportunities came along to do new and exciting things, I would sometimes forget to cherish each occasion as a blessed and stimulating experience that would inspire others to pursue passionate and purposeful lives.

When I made a choice to turn my focus to the lives that were being touched through my work, my self-imposed burdens lifted. As simple as it sounds, it was truly a revelation. I realized I could lighten up! Have fun. Enjoy my successes, large and small. The light bulb went on in my head and shed light on experiences that deserved my appreciation. I stopped minimizing my success and began enjoying it. Now the richest reward of my career is the feedback I receive from people who make positive changes in their lives as a result of something I've written or said. When I determined to notice and celebrate the milestones on my path, I realized that it's not the destination that brings fulfillment, but the sights along the way.

In *Rich Minds, Rich Rewards,* I wrote about the what's-next syndrome, the ways in which we concentrate with such intensity on what's next that we pay no attention to "what's now." A constant focus on the future keeps us from enjoying the present. Eliminating this habit is possible, but it takes practice. As your mind begins racing to anticipate what's ahead, deliberately focus on your immediate environment to bring your thoughts back to the present. Try it right now. As you read these words, notice your fingertips as they touch the pages of the book. Notice the comfort of your body as you relax and enjoy reading. Feel your lungs expand as you take each breath. Tune out the world around you and tune in to the world within. People with a light attitude always focus on the moment—the people who are with them, experiences as they happen, and the uniqueness to be found in both.

Let me give you picture of what I mean. During a recent evening walk to get my daily dose of exercise, I was so focused on my "destination"— walking a certain distance—that I barely noticed my surroundings. Then I glanced up and absorbed a moment that stopped me in my tracks. As I stood in front of a small lake surrounded by the sidewalk I had turned into my personal track, I saw that the Rocky Mountains in the distance were a steel blue-gray, their jagged edges outlined against the orangish pink sunset. The sky was mostly blue, but a string of soft pink clouds hovered at an angle over the lake, causing a magnificent reflection of pink, blue, and white over the light ripples of water. As I took in the postcard-perfect view before me, a trio of tiny brown and white ducks glided across the center of the lake. As they headed for the shore, I noticed sporadic bubbles popping to the surface of the water. Little pond fish that never quite raised their heads to the surface were making their presence known, and the resulting concentric circles moved like sound waves from the center of each bubble. The innocent laughter of children playing at the water's edge provided a perfect soundtrack for this perfect scene. Thank God I glanced up.

If we are not careful, we can get so focused on our destination that we never glance up to enjoy the beauty of our path. When we are in tune with the rhythms of life, we notice the moments worth remembering.

Stop Struggling and Start Flowing with Life

A major turning point in my life occurred the day I decided to stop struggling. Nothing changed in my circumstances, which at the time were looking rather bleak. My largest account had folded six months earlier, and I had yet to replace the revenue it generated. Mounting debt, shrinking income, and growing expenses consumed my thoughts. Fear set in. I felt an undercurrent trying to suck me under. Frustration gave way to thoughts of giving up and looking for a nine-to-five job where someone else shouldered the responsibility and pressures of keeping a business going. I was beginning to feel defeated. Something in my spirit said, "Don't give up," but with no other evidence to encourage me, I was getting close to my limit. *There must be a lesson in this,* I thought, but I didn't know what it was. So I kept busy doing what I felt was necessary to fix the situation.

As I poured out my woes over the phone to a close friend one night, she spoke just the words I needed to hear—although they were tough to swallow. "Just stop," she said. "Let God do His job and stop trying to do it for Him. You're struggling and pushing when it's your time to relax and have faith."

Upon hanging up the phone, I took a deep breath and thought about her words. Often people tell us things we already know are true. We just need to be reminded. "Let go and let God" had long been a favorite phrase of mine. Yet in this situation my words and actions reflected not trust and faith, but struggle and worry. It had been easy to let go and let God when I could see how I would stay afloat, but as my financial resources began to run dry, my faith became weak.

Proverbs 3:5-6 came to me again, "Trust in the LORD with all your heart, and lean not on your own understanding; in all your ways acknowledge Him, and He shall direct your paths." Not content to fail this test of my faith, I embraced the idea that doors open and close in our lives for a purpose, and we must trust that everything happens in perfect timing—even if it's not in *our* perfect timing.

So I prayed for direction on my path, God gave it, and I followed it. It was not new direction; it was just that I finally decided to trust God and do what He had been telling me to do for some time. His direction was not to the obvious source of revenue, so I had resisted it. It's incredible that when we don't get the answers we want to our prayers, we try things our way until we get tired of failing. I became so frustrated that I finally followed the divine direction I received. In an amazingly short period of time, my financial stress began to melt away as a result of pursuing the path God directed me to take.

Remember that your job is to go with the flow of life, even when it carries you through rough times. Rather than swimming upstream, tiring yourself out, and making the journey longer than it needs to be, let the current determine your course. Accept that life won't always be what you want it to be, but that doesn't mean you aren't headed in the right direction. Relax and have faith. Learn the lessons that only adversity can teach, so that you won't find yourself in rough waters time and time again.

Refuse to struggle in any area of your life. If a door is closed, don't struggle to pry it open. Trust that if it is meant to be, it will be. When you feel the urge to fight, take a deep breath and relax. Think of the many times you wasted energy raging against reality, only to see a problem work itself out.

Keep moving forward, doing the work that needs to be done on your divine path. Enjoy each moment as you flow with the natural rhythm of life. And glance up every so often to revel in the magnificence along your path.

❧ WALKING YOUR PATH ❧

Listen to Your Life: Go with the Flow

Place a check mark in front of every statement that is true for you.

____ My friends and family would describe me as someone who "goes with the flow."

____ There is nothing regularly draining my energy (such as negative relationships, ongoing financial problems, a job I dislike, etc.).

____ There is no one in my life—past or present—I have not forgiven.

____ I do not procrastinate.

____ I have learned at least one valuable lesson from every trial I have endured.

____ I am patient about my vision, fully trusting God's timing in bringing it to fruition.

____ I have allowed purpose to be birthed through the pain and challenges I have experienced in my life.

____ In the past year I have expanded my capacity to handle more of what my life has to offer.

____ My life is not weighed down with constant worry or self-imposed pressure.

____ I am able to desire something without being overly attached to it. I hold my dreams loosely.

____ I am fully enjoying my journey!

If you checked off most or all of the above statements, the principle of flow is already at work in your life. If you didn't check any of the statements, don't be discouraged. You have the ability to change your attitude and begin flowing with the current of your life.

5-Minute Action Step

Carve out five minutes today to identify several challenges that are blocking your ability to flow with life. Everyone's path is filled with challenges, though some are more painful or difficult than others. Living the life you were born to live requires the ability to learn from those trials and continue moving on your path.

    1.

    2.

    3.

    4.

    5.

48-Hour Challenge

In the next two days, challenge yourself to address at least one of the issues identified in your "five-minute action step." Take action to overcome the challenge in some tangible way. If you need to forgive someone, take the necessary steps to do so. If you have been ignoring your intuition about a particular issue, take action. If something is draining your energy, take steps to eliminate the problem. Once you have eliminated one challenge, set a date to overcome the next challenge until you are completely free to flow on your path the way God intended.

✑ PRAYER OF FLOW ✐

I pray that I will always listen to my life and trust that "all things work together for good to those who love God...[and] are the called according to His purpose." ^{Romans 8:28} *Help me remember that everything happens for a reason. I want to learn the lesson in every experience, Lord. Teach me. Give me the ability to learn and grow quickly so that I may move into the greater purpose You have for me. I do not want to repeat the same lessons over and over again. Wherever tragedy has occurred in my life, help me gain treasure from it. Wherever there is pain, allow purpose to prevail. Help me replace worry with worship so that I do not take my focus away from You in times of trouble but instead turn to You as my source of strength and resilience. I understand that dealing with difficult circumstances on my path tests my faith. Give me the wisdom to allow it to produce patience in me. Your Word says, "Count it all joy when you fall into various trials, knowing that the testing of your faith produces patience. But let patience have its perfect work, that you may be perfect and complete, lacking nothing."* ^{James 1:2-4} *I praise You for being a God of purpose. I praise You for all You have brought me through and all You have in store for me as I pass the tests of life. Amen.*

ABUNDANCE

Believing That Everything You Need Is Available to You

He who sows sparingly will also reap sparingly,
and he who sows bountifully will also reap bountifully.
—2 CORINTHIANS 9:6

We live in a limitless universe—abundant beyond human comprehension. Yet most people resist the concept that the possibilities for abundance in their lives are limitless. They limit God and how much they can be blessed. They continually labor to make ends meet. They struggle in love, in their careers, health, finances, and other key areas of life. Their futile efforts serve only to reinforce their belief that existing resources cannot meet their needs and that they must fight for the little they hope to obtain. They resist the idea that abundance can and does exist, if only they will seek it and embrace it.

An unhealthy attitude permeates our society, an attitude that declares,

"What you have is not enough." Advertisers have trained us to believe that in order to be happy, we need the things their companies have to offer—or at least what they represent. We *need* the latest sleek sport utility vehicle, not because we like it more than all the other options, but because it will somehow give us the "right" image. Fashion magazines tell us we need to update our wardrobes to reflect the latest trends if we really want to capture attention at work or in the dating scene. The not-enough attitude is not limited to consumerism. It shapes our views toward love and money and looks. We believe we can never have quite enough of the "right" things to be truly satisfied.

I call this attitude of discontentment a "lack mentality." A lack mentality is a thought pattern in which you consistently focus on deficiencies—real or perceived. Rather than enjoying the abundance of the good already present in your life, you focus on what is missing, what is wrong, or what is not perfect.

A lack mentality believes that there is not enough to go around and that we are all fighting for a scarce supply of money, love, jobs, business, friends, family, and anything else in the world we want. Someone with this mentality sees everyone as competition and maintains a negative outlook on even the simplest aspects of life.

Those who experience extraordinary success know that practicing an attitude of abundance—focusing on what you have and what you would like to see manifested in your life—is the antidote to the lack mentality. Remember that what you focus on will expand. This is just as true for the principle of abundance as it is for vision or flow. If you focus on what you don't have, it is likely that you will continue to create more struggles with that issue. On the other hand, believing in the possibility of abundance in your life is the first step to experiencing it. It's one of the greatest universal truths: You will reap what you sow.

The apostle Paul certainly knew a great deal about abundance. This man, whose letters comprise more than half of the Bible's New Testament, wrote from a prison cell about being content no matter his circumstances (see Philippians 4:11). In another letter he described God as being "able to do exceedingly abundantly above all that we ask or think, according to the power that works in us" (Ephesians 3:20). What an incredible promise! Just think about it for a moment: "exceedingly abundantly above all that we [could *ever*] ask or think." It's as though Paul were saying that God already knows that you limit your thinking. You may limit what is possible for your life, but God does not. No matter what you ask, God can exceed it.

RECOGNIZING THE ABUNDANT POSSIBILITIES

Apart from knowing that you are living your mission in life, perhaps the most exciting part of walking on your path is that the possibilities for success are limitless. The path to the life you were born to live leads to more blessings and fulfilling opportunities than any other path you can choose. The path God created for you is the path of greatest abundance. You can choose another path, but you will always know in your spirit that something is missing and life has more to offer. Perhaps even more of a tragedy, your natural gifts and talents will not be fully expressed.

Why do so many people disregard or overlook the abundant possibilities their lives offer?

- They have not been exposed to anything greater than what currently exists in their lives, and their vision for life's possibilities is limited to what they have already experienced.
- They lack confidence that their natural gifts and talents could be used in a significant way.

- They refuse to get in sync with God's timing. For example, you might believe you can earn more money—and earn it faster—by chasing success on another path. Often, there is much more money available on your true path, but it is available only in God's timing.
- They are so used to struggling to get what they want and need that the concept of having everything available to them seems like a dream.

Those who consider themselves spiritual often shy away from the topic of abundance, in part because they associate the term *abundance* only with money, and they associate money with evil. Abundance includes but is not limited to money. Abundance applies to any area of your life that is important to your spiritual, physical, and mental well-being. That could include good health, happiness, opportunities to fulfill your life mission, love, family, meaningful friendships, spiritual growth, and yes, financial prosperity.

Of course, what use is an abundance of money if you lack love, joy, or peace of mind? Money won't deliver those priceless gifts. It will, however, give you the freedom and comfort to enjoy certain experiences, to say no to something that you might not say no to otherwise, or to bless others in tremendous ways. One of the most fulfilling aspects of having money is that you can have a positive impact on the lives and causes you care about. Surely, financial blessings are not solely about our personal pleasure, but they give us greater opportunities to fulfill our divine mission.

Take some time now to answer the following questions and explore your beliefs about abundance:

1. Do you believe that all of your needs can be met? Or do you believe that you will always want for something?

2. If you believe that you will always want for something, what is it that you feel you will always lack in your life? Or what have you always lacked in your life?

3. I invite you to open your mind to the idea that everything you want and need is available to you. For a few moments, close your eyes and meditate on this idea. Imagine living a life in which everything you want and need is available in abundance. What do you see? What do you most want in abundance in your life?

4. What's stopping you from having an abundance of it right now?

Through your actions, you can choose to attract those possibilities to yourself or to repel them. You won't necessarily find abundance overnight, but in due course your path will lead you to the richest rewards as you adopt the practices we'll discuss in this chapter: embracing an attitude of thankfulness, using what you already have, expanding your knowledge base, and creating an environment that attracts more of what you want.

Embracing an Attitude of Thankfulness

Abundance begins with your attitude toward life. Do you see life as a succession of struggles and hard work in an unfair world of "haves" and "have-nots"? Or do you see it as a precious gift and a journey of lessons? The

What Your Life Is Saying About Abundance

How do you know if you are operating from a lack mentality?

- You compare what everyone else has with what you have, even if you have more.
- You believe there is a limit to how much good can come into your life.
- You focus on what you do not have rather than counting the blessings of what you do have.
- You never seem to be able to generate enough income, save enough money, or keep enough money to feel you are living an abundant life.
- You feel that you do not have a choice about your circumstances.
- Your energy is depleted.
- Fear holds you back from letting go of old clutter, old relationships, old ideas, and old problems.
- You regularly run out of household items.
- You squeeze so much into your day that you rarely arrive on time for appointments.

What are the signs that you've put the principle of abundance to work in your life?

second view inspires an attitude of thankfulness, which is an important step in abundant living.

If you want to experience a new level of joy, try cultivating the habit of being thankful for every blessing in your life. When I say "every blessing," I truly mean *every* blessing. Look around you right now. What do you have in this moment to be thankful for? How about life, breath, light, strength, and sight? What about the things for which you have perhaps never given thanks, such as your computer, clothes, bathtub, books, telephone,

- You have a reserve of everything you need: love, space, money, energy, and healthy relationships.
- You are not anxious about getting what you want or need.
- You are consistently filled with energy that empowers you to live fully every day.
- You currently have the resources to live comfortably for at least one year without working.
- You have no consumer debt (credit cards, student loans, or other installment debt).
- You feel that you have as much space as you need in your home, car, and work environment.
- You get plenty of rest every night.
- Your work offers you an opportunity to succeed and fulfill your purpose.
- You regularly invest your time in activities that will reap rewards in the future.
- You have the help you need to get important things done.
- You have positive, supportive relationships with friends and family who love you and demonstrate that love through their actions.
- You have a strong and growing relationship with God.

photographs, or bed? What if you were truly thankful for everything in your life—even for the people or things that aggravate you?

For example, when my mother lost her ability to swallow after suffering a stroke, the doctors inserted a feeding tube into her stomach. For months my mother prayed that her ability to swallow would be restored so that the tube could be removed. But even as she prayed for healing, she was always thankful for the tube that enabled her to receive nourishment and to regain strength as well as the weight she had lost.

When you are thankful for every blessing, large and small, you begin your journey into abundance. You awaken your mind to what is often missed because you spend so much of life focusing on the things you feel are somehow missing. The truth is, until you awaken to the wonderful things already present in your life, you are not ready to experience a higher level of abundance. If you cannot see and appreciate the abundance that exists in your life today, you will never be satisfied.

The man who believes his life will be complete when he makes his first million will find something missing when he reaches his goal. Either the million dollars will not be enough and he will strive for more, or he will transfer his perception of what is missing to some other area of his life. Perhaps he'll suddenly be dissatisfied with his marriage, begin an affair, get a divorce, and remarry. But when a new wife doesn't meet all of his needs, he'll think that what he really needs is a fancy sports car...or a boat...or whatever. An absence of thankfulness nearly always leads to a lack mentality.

Deliberately choosing gratitude, however, can transform a dismal outlook into one of hopeful optimism, as one of my clients discovered. Diana, a single and professionally successful engineer, had been laid off from her six-figure job eight months earlier. Her hopes of landing a comparable position had been dashed repeatedly, and she was relying primarily on short-term consulting projects for her income. The projects generated approximately 30 percent of the monthly salary she had been earning, and there were no benefits.

At first she expressed anger and frustration about her situation. But I challenged her to consider what she had to be thankful for: the income from her consulting, a background and education that would eventually help her land a new position, savings that helped cushion the financial blow, and loved ones who were supportive and loving during a difficult time. As we talked, Diana determined to focus on the blessings in her life rather than on what she lacked.

She decided that there was a lesson for her to learn through her experience, and she determined not to miss it, whatever it might be. Ultimately, she learned that she was a survivor, that her job did not define her worth, and that she valued having free time more than she enjoyed the money she'd been making while working a schedule determined by someone else. The layoff gave her the space to think and determine what mattered most in her life. The lessons she learned were not revealed until she embraced an attitude of thankfulness, which empowered her to see the abundance that existed in her life despite her lack of money.

Use What You've Been Given

What gift have you received? Perhaps it is the flair to entertain or inspire. Perhaps it is the ability to fix things, cook well, or serve others with a smile. You may be a "techie" who is great at finding solutions to problems or programming software. Maybe you have the gift of creating beauty, connecting people, or making others laugh. Whatever your gift, you have a responsibility to be a good steward of it: "As each one has received a gift, minister it to one another, as good stewards of the manifold grace of God" (1 Peter 4:10).

Investing in your talent by learning, growing, and positively impacting others illustrates good stewardship. Remember Matthew 25:21: "Well done, good and faithful servant; you were faithful over a few things, I will make you ruler over many things. Enter into the joy of your lord."

You have everything you need to experience abundance, but you must acknowledge your gifts and use them fully. Imagine a world in which every person used his or her unique gift to minister to others. That would be a perfect world—each person providing just what another needed at just the perfect moment.

Good stewards not only *use* their gifts and multiply their rewards, but they also take care of what they have been given, no matter how seemingly small. Do you treat yourself, your talents, money, relationships, and material possessions with the utmost respect and care? If not, you may find yourself struggling to obtain more of something for which you have not proven to be a good steward. If, for example, you waste your money and do not handle it responsibly, why should you be blessed with more? You will likely find that when you begin respecting and effectively managing whatever you have been blessed with, more will begin flowing abundantly into your life.

Share Your Blessings Freely

Our society encourages us in every situation to ask, What can I get out of this? What's in it for me? We are taught to focus on what we can get from people, jobs, opportunities, and situations. Those who assume this attitude believe the world revolves around them and that they can never have enough.

The reverse of this involves focusing on what you can give to others. When you acknowledge the abundance of resources and gifts in your life and what you have to offer, you begin to ask the question, What can I give? This question reveals the richness of your life and the clarity of your perspective. It expresses an attitude of love and contentment—love toward others and yourself and contentment in your circumstances and with what you have to offer. Focusing on what you have to give empowers you to make decisions that are in line with your divine path. Why? Because when you recognize the gifts you have been given and commit to expressing them, you find yourself taking actions that fulfill your purpose.

Second Corinthians 9:6-8 tells us,

He who sows sparingly will also reap sparingly, and he who sows bountifully will also reap bountifully. So let each one give as he purposes in his heart, not grudgingly or of necessity; for God loves a cheerful giver. And God is able to make all grace abound toward you, that you, always having all sufficiency in all things, have an abundance for every good work.

In other words, the gifts you've been given are not yours to keep but yours to share. Allow God's love to flow through you to others. This is the ultimate meeting of the three levels of connection—God, you, and others. Just as God works through others to bless you, be consistently open to ways in which God can work through you to bless others.

When you focus on what you can give, you naturally attract blessings in abundance. The door you open to give generously to others is the same door through which you can receive. When you close the door to giving, you close the door to receiving in abundance. This rule of life applies to every area in which you seek abundance—love, finances, joy, career, family peace, trusting friendships. In healthy relationships, when you focus on acceptance and appreciation and giving love, you tend to receive more of the same in return. In finances, when you're willing to help others while practicing good stewardship of your resources, you find that your own needs are met more often.

When you want to experience joy, focus on creating and contributing to joyful experiences and sharing a joyful attitude with those you encounter.

In your career, focus on using your gifts and talents in ways that benefit the greater cause of the organization without worrying about what you want in return. This generosity and dedication will tend to attract an abundance of opportunities into your path, whether through your current employer or through some other source.

To experience an abundance of peace in your family and other relationships, focus on being peaceful and loving, even in the midst of chaos and turmoil. Answer negativity with love.

To enjoy an abundance of trustworthy friendships, be a trustworthy friend.

No matter what you are seeking, focus on what you already have to give in that area of your life. Proverbs 11:25 promises, "The generous soul will be made rich, and he who waters will also be watered himself."

Fall in Love with Your Work

When it comes to work, many people do not believe that God will bless them with an abundance of the work they love. For them, work is hard and not enjoyable. Perhaps you are one of the "Thank God it's Friday" crowd. For this group, work that doesn't feel like work would seem frivolous!

Whether you work on Wall Street or your street, you likely spend at least one-third of your time working. If that time is spent on work you cannot stand, it will be impossible to experience abundance. Abundance is about "feeling full" or "fulfilled." The most abundant work path is the one that uses your natural talents and gifts. The doors of abundance open widest in the direction of your talents. In an abundant life, the work you do is an extension of who you are. It helps you fulfill your purpose and impact lives in a powerful way, as only you can because of your unique talents.

Whatever you love doing, there is an opportunity to make a living at it. Your job is to make that opportunity a reality. Don't allow a lack mentality to blind you to opportunities to do what you love or convince you that leaving a job to launch a dream business is risky. In my view, the possibility that a business may fail or a dream may not come to fruition is not a risk worth worrying about. The biggest risk is that you will arrive at the end of your days and realize that your fear of failure caused you to waste the precious gift of life.

An old song came to mind while I was writing about doing what you love. One line goes something like this: "If you can't be with the one you love, honey, love the one you're with." If you find yourself resisting what you love, and you choose to keep doing something that does not nourish your spirit, then at the very least, make a decision to love what you do. You may not enjoy your job or the people with whom you work, but you have a choice about your attitude toward the job. A mind-set of abundance creates a joyful attitude that embraces the power of choice. If you choose not to do the work you love, then choose to "love the work you're with."

EXPANDING YOUR BASE OF KNOWLEDGE

"You don't know what you don't know and you think you know," speaker Les Brown often points out.

Perhaps nothing is more stifling to your potential than thinking that you already know everything you need to know. The very essence of the principle of abundance is that your possibilities are infinite. If your possibilities are infinite, then there must always be something you haven't yet learned—even if you are at the height of your success.

What is it that you don't yet know? Even more important, what don't you even know that you don't know? To answer this question, open yourself to exploring new ideas and listening to other people. You may be very knowledgeable in several areas, but you can learn something from absolutely everyone.

We live in an information-hungry society. As a result, opportunities often flock to those who are information-rich. This is one of the many reasons why education is so important. Knowing the "how-tos" of life strengthens your ability to attract more of what you want. While formal education is certainly valuable, what makes you most attractive is your attitude and your willingness to learn and try knew things. Success comes to those with a thirst for knowledge, ideas, and concepts beyond their current knowledge base.

Whether in your career, love life, friendships and family relationships, finances, or health, increasing your understanding about how to improve the quality and effectiveness of what you do will make various aspects of your life more successful. You'll begin to grasp the full scope of options for your life. Where you once faced tremendous obstacles, you'll now see challenges that you can work through with confidence or avoid altogether. This is why people hire coaches, consultants, and therapists. It is the reason you are reading this book right now—to expand your base of knowledge.

Let's take, for example, the area of personal finances. Marcus deter-

---

Building on What You Know

How do the previous six principles help you "reap bountifully"?

1. *Connection.* When you seek God's presence in your life, abundance will follow. You must abide with Him, spending time in His presence and seeking His goodness, purpose, and ways. "If you abide in Me, and My words abide in you, you will ask what you desire, and it shall be done for you. By this My Father is glorified, that you bear much fruit," Jesus told the disciples (John 15:7-8).
2. *Self-curiosity.* By diligently seeking to eliminate the issues that hold you back and learn from your own emotions, you remove the weeds that threaten to choke the potential harvest.

---

mined that one of his life goals is to enjoy financial abundance. The idea
sounded exciting but rather foreign to him. Born into a hard-working,
stable middle-class family, he was encouraged to go to school, get a good
job with a large company, and save his money. Marcus graduated from
college, landed a respectable position as a financial analyst for a major
bank, was promoted twice, and consistently saved 15 percent of his income for seven years. Even so, he could see that his dream of financial
freedom would be decades away at this rate. How could he accelerate his
path to financial freedom?

By seeking the answer to that question, Marcus began to expand his
knowledge base about wealth building. He had never personally known
anyone who had successfully found financial independence, nor had he
considered any financial strategies beyond those in his circle of knowledge: Get a job and save money. Once he committed to increasing his
knowledge of the subject, Marcus experienced a new level of excitement.
He learned that he needed to increase his streams of revenue, and he

3. *Vision*. The vision of fulfillment in your life is a picture of abundance.
   It illustrates what life will look and feel like when you begin living
   your purpose daily.
4. *Creativity*. Creativity taps into the abundance of God's creation and
   the limitless ways in which your vision can be accomplished. It
   requires you to dig deep within your spirit to open the treasure chest
   of ideas that is waiting there.
5. *Expectancy*. When you begin expecting more, you will take action
   based on that expectation. Your action sows seeds that will bear fruit.
6. *Flow*. Moving with the current of life empowers you to increase your
   capacity to give and receive. It stretches and expands your path,
   enabling you to maximize the opportunities that flow into your path.

concluded that real-estate investing would be a wise strategy to help him attract financial success. He positioned himself to accomplish his goals by launching a business, taking real-estate classes, and starting to accumulate rental properties. According to plan, he is on track to achieve financial freedom in ten years. Success was waiting for him, but he had to be willing to stretch his thinking.

As you seek new avenues for receiving the abundance available to you, consider these questions:

- What area of your life is slow to attract the type of success you would love to have?
- What one step could you take today to expand your base of knowledge in that area?
- What have you always wanted to learn about?
- What is the biggest problem in your life right now? What skills would help you solve it?

Expanding your base of knowledge opens your eyes to the multitude of options for a fulfilling life. You can gather new ideas by connecting with other people and exposing yourself to worlds beyond your current experience.

Connect to People with Other Ideas

As you seek to increase your knowledge, pay attention to others who have achieved a higher level of success. What could you learn from them? If you want to boost your success, what steps can you take to make your path wider and smoother—allowing for greater abundance with minimal effort? The couple whose marriage is consistently strong and healthy is doing something different from the couple that always seems to be in strife. If your goal is a successful marriage, notice what you are doing or not doing compared to couples who are in obviously healthy relationships. The real estate agent who earns $500,000 per year has the same number of hours in her day as the agent who earns $50,000 per year. If your goal is to increase your income, study the steps that will allow you to multiply your income by replacing old habits with ones that work better for you.

Listen to people who know what they're talking about—and don't argue with them. So many people refuse to accept any advice that does not fit their limited reality. Rather than thinking, *Hey, maybe my way* isn't *the only way,* they insist that anyone who suggests ideas unfamiliar to them is somehow misguided, untrustworthy, or living in a dream world. The latter is often true. Those with different ideas are in a dream world, but they've translated their dreams into reality. Pay attention to those who are willing to share their hard-won wisdom, even if you feel that your circumstances are so different from theirs that there is nothing of value for you to learn. A person does not have to come from precisely the same background as you or have the same experience for you to learn from them. If you find it challenging to learn from others, practice a healthy dose of self-curiosity about this issue. Why do you resist ideas if they are not yours? Why do you believe no one but you can know the answers?

Self-curiosity is a key to extraordinary success—and so is a healthy curiosity about the success of others. Don't be afraid to ask questions of other successful people. Learn from them. You do not even have to speak to people one-on-one to glean wisdom and inspiration from them. You can be mentored through their work, their biographies, their attitudes, and their legacies.

Expose Yourself to a New World

When I was in second grade, my father was given the choice of being assigned to an Air Force base in one of three locations: New York, Hawaii, or Germany.

"Where would you like to go?" I recall my parents asking me.

"Oh, that's easy," I said, recalling the action-packed episodes of *Hawaii Five-O* I enjoyed watching at my grandparents' house. "Hawaii!" I pictured myself inside one of those episodes, on a beach with waves even bigger than the ones we enjoyed in Florida. I could hear the theme song playing in my head.

My parents looked at each other for a moment, then turned back to me.

"Well, what do you think about Germany?" my dad asked, clearly steering me in the direction he and my mother were leaning.

"Germany? Where's that?" I said with a frown, a bit puzzled that they weren't as excited about Hawaii as I was. It seemed like a no-brainer in my little mind.

"Germany is another country," my dad explained. "It's in Europe, and we could drive to France, England, Belgium, and a lot of other countries in just a few hours," he added in an energetic, persuasive tone.

I countered with attempts to be equally persuasive about Hawaii, but to no avail. A few months later, my parents and I moved to Frankfurt, West Germany, as it was called then. I marveled at how different it was from the only world I had ever known. I am sure Hawaii would have been beautiful, but I am grateful that my parents chose Germany.

Everything was different—the cars, the language, the culture. It was the late seventies, and I called it "the little car country" because I had never seen so many small cars. I was used to big American models. Then there were the people. In my limited experience, I imagined that all people who were not from the United States looked like people from China. Don't ask me where I got that idea! Imagine my surprise upon our arrival.

By the age of nine, I had traveled all over Germany, Switzerland, Holland, and France. I began learning German and continued to do so through college. My adventures included visiting thousand-year-old castles, struggling to communicate with people who spoke a different language, and recognizing that across nationalities and language, people are just people. It piqued my interest in other cultures and languages, which prompted me to later learn Spanish and earn a degree in International Affairs.

My exposure to a new world led me down a path that turned toward new possibilities. There is a feeling of abundance that comes from experiencing life outside of your piece of the world. Suddenly the world becomes a much bigger place, and you gain perspective on your role in it. In contrast, when you never venture beyond your own little piece of the world, you can stifle your ability to fully experience abundance.

As you seek to gain new knowledge, expose yourself to different cultures, people, ideas, and possibilities. Try something you have never done before. How can you determine what you want in life if you have not been exposed to all of your options? So much is available to you, but you have only so much time to experience it. Physical travel to faraway places is not your only option. Travel to a new world through books, classes, or surfing the Internet. Visit places around the country, in your own state, or just across the railroad tracks. Don't limit your context to the world you see every day.

CREATING AN ENVIRONMENT THAT ATTRACTS MORE OF WHAT YOU WANT

Sometimes when abundance comes our way, we're not prepared to make the most of it. Perhaps we're overwhelmed by the demands of life, or we simply haven't cleared away enough of the unimportant things to make room to enjoy the privileges that are ours for the taking. Whatever you want to attract more of—love, financial success, business growth, creative ideas—take some simple steps so that you'll be ready to welcome it wholeheartedly.

Seize Your Window of Opportunity

Often, opportunities that come our way are time sensitive. That is why it is critical to live with some sense of urgency. Those who keep their eyes open for opportunities, then take advantage of them when they arise, are most likely to tap into their potential for abundance.

Consider my mother's example. After she suffered a massive stroke and lost such abilities as walking, talking, swallowing, clear vision, and balance, she determined to focus on recovery. Unable to continue her previous career due to her disabilities, she spends a great deal of time at home during the day. She has made it her mission to stretch herself beyond what would be expected of a person with her physical challenges. She chooses not to wait for others to do things for her. And she continually pushes herself to do more, standing long enough to cook a meal, practicing walking slowly down the driveway without a cane, or riding an extra few minutes on the stationary bicycle. She understands that if she does not focus on strengthening the abilities she has, she may lose them forever. She describes it as her use-it-or-lose-it philosophy.

"I figure that if I keep on practicing, I will eventually get better," she told me once. She is right. She has made remarkable progress one step at a time by practicing the things she finds difficult until she can do them very well. "The more I do it, the easier it becomes," she explains.

In watching this process, I have seen her go from not being able to sit up to learning to use a wheelchair. I've witnessed her progress from walking with a walker to using a cane to walking all by herself. I have watched her go from being completely unable to swallow to drinking liquids, from eating puréed foods to having the feeding tube removed from her stomach. Little by little, in every area affected by the stroke, she has worked hard to fulfill her potential and regain the use of her body.

The key in her recovery, which continues as I write, is taking advantage of the window of opportunity. Certain opportunities in life exist only for a limited time. We either use the opportunity or lose it. What opportunity do you need to seize?

Karen left her position with an established company to start her own advertising agency. Extremely creative and talented, she found herself struggling to keep up with the demand for her services. It was time to expand her business, but she was afraid to hire the help she needed. Opportunities flowed into her path, but because she was overwhelmed with doing all of the work herself, she did not take advantage of them. When she came to me for coaching, she was overworked and upset with herself for letting so many opportunities pass her by.

I invited her to first forgive herself for missing some opportunities and commend herself for stepping out on faith to use her talents to do what she loves for a living. It is important to acknowledge the steps forward that you take. It is equally important to accept that you are human. You will not do anything perfectly, but when you learn from your mistakes and make changes based on what you learn, you move further down your path.

"Clearly you are overworked, Karen. What do you want to do about it?" I asked her.

"I would like to hire the help I need, but I am afraid that I will not have the money to meet the demands of a payroll," she answered, sounding stressed and frantic.

"Do your financial projections support hiring someone?" I probed.

There was a long pause. "Well, I don't have any projections," she admitted. "And I need to meet with my accountant. I've been so busy trying to do the work that I haven't done any planning, and I'm afraid it's going to cost too much to get my accountant involved."

Karen was basing her business and financial decisions on her fear of not having enough. Her lack mentality prevented her from embracing the abundant opportunities that were flowing into her path. After a few coaching sessions, and with the support and financial information she needed, Karen finally mustered the courage to hire her first employee. With the time that was freed up from her schedule, she began contacting some of the companies that had approached her. A few had found other agencies to handle their needs—remember the use-it-or-lose-it principle—but a few of them were still very interested in working with her.

Remember, seize opportunities when they come, but even if you miss them when they initially cross your path, it never hurts to see if the door might still be open.

Clear Space to Welcome the Abundant Life

Often, we seek new opportunities, relationships, and blessings in our lives, but we don't make room for those desires to manifest themselves. When your life is cluttered with old, stale habits, relationships, and situations, you prevent fresh, new, and desirable things and people from showing up. Relationships tend to be an area in which people's lives are consistently cluttered, as they allow certain people to drain their energy indefinitely. There may be some friendships you simply need to let go of, while other relationships will require deliberate action to limit their negative impact on your energy level.

Here are five suggestions for spring cleaning your life:

1. *List ten things you are putting up with in your life.* These can be anything from the broken appliances that irritate you every time you have to use them to the high-cholesterol diet you have been meaning to change.

2. *Make requests and take action to clear these things from your life.* A list is only beneficial if you allow it to move you to *action.* From the list you developed, write down the actions and requests you need to make in order to clear these ten things out of your life. Then make it happen!

3. *Clear your clutter in the three physical environments that affect you most.* Clutter drains your energy and decreases your effectiveness. Have you ever noticed that after you clean off your desk you feel that you can conquer your work?

4. *Hire people to support you.* It is important to put support systems in place so that you don't overload your life, leaving no room for an abundance of the things you want and enjoy most. Ask yourself this question, What are the things that I do not enjoy doing that I can hire someone to assist with? Make a list, then prioritize your budget so that you can pay for the help you need, whether it be a housekeeper, a baby-sitter, a CPA, a personal trainer, lawn service, pet service, or an auto detailer.

5. *Be willing to let go.* What are you holding on to that doesn't serve your life in a healthy way any longer? Don't allow fear to keep you holding on to things and situations in your life that are no longer positive and useful. Either take action to revive them or let them go altogether, believing that as you let go, you will make room for something better to come along.

Keep in mind that your physical environment is often reflective of your mental state. If you found this to-do list overwhelming, it may be because you need to give special attention to step 3: clearing the clutter from your physical environments.

Few people are able to relax or focus in a messy, chaotic environment with unattractive colors and decor. While trying to relax, you may begin to think about what you don't like, what needs to be cleaned, and the clutter that needs to be cleared away. Just as the beauty and order of a luxurious hotel can stimulate your senses, clutter can do the opposite. It brings down your energy level and contributes to feelings of being overwhelmed or stuck. I have even heard clients talk about feeling claustrophobic in their own home or office.

The process of clearing clutter is often a catalyst for moving forward, and it is also a catalyst for creating the feeling that you have space in your life.

In general, there are four different types of clutter: (1) too much stuff in too little space, (2) things you don't like or use anymore that are taking up space, (3) messy and disorganized spaces, and (4) unfinished projects. If you have any of these types of clutter, schedule some time in the next week to clear it away so that you can maximize the effectiveness and beauty of your environments—at home, at work, and in your car.

Upon clearing the clutter, it is always a treat to unveil surroundings of beauty and inspiration. My writing room is both practical and inspiring, filled with romantic artwork—all in black and white. Views of Paris rest over the fireplace. A kissing couple hangs over a cozy, cream-colored love seat draped with a soft, dark afghan. Arranged on my desk are long-stemmed roses and pictures that remind me of my love for writing and the power of words. The balcony door gives way to the soothing sound of a waterfall that bubbles outside. When I feel stuck in my writing, I lie back on the love seat and rest. In the beauty of this peaceful space, inspiration always comes.

What would add beauty to your environment?

As you make room in your life for what you want, you will soon find that what you want most is attracted to you. And you'll be ready to embrace an abundance of opportunities and success.

If you sow into your unique and divinely ordained path by doing the things we have talked about in this book, you *will* reap an abundant harvest in your life. Each principle connects in order to bring you to a place of abundance, a place of truly extraordinary success, where you are fulfilled in the most important ways.

❧ WALKING YOUR PATH ❧

Listen to Your Life: Are You Enjoying an Abundant Life?

Place a check mark in front of every statement that is true for you.

____ I always feel that I have enough of what I need.

____ I always feel that I have enough of what I want.

____ There is nothing else I would rather be doing than the work I do now.

____ My marriage (or significant love relationship) is fulfilling.

____ I have personal friendships with a variety of people, including people who differ from me professionally, geographically, politically, financially, racially, and intellectually.

____ I believe with all of my heart that my family and I can create and live a life of true abundance.

____ I consider it a privilege and a joy to give of my money and other resources to help people and causes I care about.

____ I take full advantage of the opportunities that cross my path.

____ I have all the love I want in my life.

____ Phrases such as "I'm broke" or "I'll never be able to afford that" are simply not in my vocabulary.

____ I am an excellent steward of my gifts and talents and fully use them to serve others.

If you had trouble checking off any of the above statements, develop a plan to create an abundant life. This will require a shift in mind-set and behavior, but it is a shift that you can make simply by choosing to do so.

5-Minute Action Step

Carve out five minutes today to identify twenty blessings in your life. Consider this a jump-start to focusing on what you do have and the possibilities that lie ahead rather than worrying about what you don't have. I challenge you to continue your list in your journal by coming up with at least one hundred blessings. Why so many? Because we are operating in abundance, of course!

1.
2.
3.
4.
5.
6.
7.
8.
9.
10.
11.
12.
13.
14.
15.
16.
17.
18.
19.
20.

48-Hour Challenge

In the next two days, make room for what you want in your life. What do you need to get rid of? Clutter on your desk or dresser? Activities on your schedule that no longer serve you? Perhaps you need to end a negative friendship or set a date by which you would like to exit your current job. Make a list of the ways in which you could make room for the things you want to show up in your life in abundance. Then get moving!

⚜ PRAYER OF ABUNDANCE ⚜

Lord, thank You for the abundance of blessings You have bestowed upon me this day. Every day of my life, You have blessed me, and I want to thank You right now for being so good. Thank You for life, love, and opportunities large and small. Thank You for the seemingly small things I take for granted because I have never had to go without them. Help me see the abundance that exists in my life today and enable me to comprehend the exceeding abundance that awaits me on my path. Free me of small thinking and from the fear that comes from focusing on lack. Show me how to build a foundation by being faithful over the things that are in my life right now. Give me a strong desire and the motivation to be an excellent steward over the gifts and resources You have given me. I understand that by being faithful with a few things, I demonstrate to You my ability to be a "ruler over many things." Matthew 25:21 *I do not want to bury my gifts, so please help me multiply them and bless others in the process. Your Word says that You will supply all of my needs according to Your riches in glory by Christ Jesus.* Philippians 4:19 *Replace all greed, stinginess, and materialism with generosity, thankfulness, and good stewardship. Help me to give easily and cheerfully. And give me the wisdom to know what to keep, what to invest, and what to give away. In times of need, help me exercise my faith and be anxious for nothing. I trust You not only to supply my needs but to give me the desires of my heart.* Psalm 37:4 *Thank You for the promises of Your Word! Now help me renew my mind and take action that will lead to an abundance of everything You meant for me to have. Amen.*

STEP FORWARD INTO YOUR DESTINY

I t is no coincidence that our paths have crossed. I believe you were guided to this book for a purpose. Perhaps it has confirmed what you know in your spirit and will serve as the extra push to move you forward on the path that's been calling you. Perhaps you were wondering how to find your path and stay on it. Whatever your situation, please don't finish this book and go back to business as usual!

An abundance of everything you want and need to walk onto your path awaits you. But you must first make the decision to find and walk your path with determination and fearlessness. You have the tools now to do that, and most important, you know how to listen to your life so that you can make the decisions that will transform it. That information comes from your connection with God, who whispers and guides you when you are quiet enough to listen. It also comes from yourself, when you take the time to get to know what's important to you, love yourself fully, and embrace your natural gifts and talents. The information you need also comes through people who cross your path daily and communicates messages you need to hear.

Will you make a decision right now to take action on what you've read?

As you move forward into a life of success far greater than you've previously believed possible, keep these strategies in mind:

- *Take steps daily.* The path to extraordinary success is a daily walk. It is a journey, not a destination to be reached at some future point in time. Success is a habit formed by the actions you take on a daily basis. Let your priorities be determined by your values, and make sure that the things you do daily are the things that matter most.

- *Embrace the opportunity to grow.* When you stretch beyond your comfort zone, you increase your capacity for higher levels of success, joy, and fulfillment. Growth is a sign of life. You will tap into your highest potential when you maximize every challenge and opportunity and overcome each obstacle—and you'll become a better person in the process.

- *Persevere!* Success does not necessarily find those who have the most talent, the best ideas, the most advantageous upbringing, or the most impressive education. Success finds those who have a plan and stick to it. You've created your vision and you know your divinely inspired purpose. Now use them as your guides. Don't abandon what you know simply because things don't work out in your timing. There are no shortcuts. Stay on your path! You will never find greater success anywhere else.

I wrote this book because I believe you can achieve your highest potential by walking your own unique path. I wanted to help you find that path and learn how to follow it toward success. You now have all the tools you need to experience the extraordinary life for which you were created.

When you stray from that path, allow *connection* to guide you back.

When the challenges seem too great, employ *self-curiosity* as a means of pressing forward.

When distractions cloud your vision, remember to focus on the smaller goals and opportunities that lie directly before you. It is the many small goals that comprise the greater *vision*.

When the obvious options simply won't work, tap into the power of *creativity* to blaze a trail to your vision. However creative you think you are—or aren't—a measure of creativity lies dormant in your spirit. Awaken it and use it.

When success seems elusive, move forward with an attitude of *expectancy*. Be sure your daily actions are aligned with the vision you have created for an extraordinary life.

When the twists and turns of life threaten to throw you off course, *flow* through them by learning and growing from your experiences—and trusting God to bring you through.

And as you live the life you were born to live, remember to open yourself to the *abundance* of all that is available to you. Be a blessing to others and watch the rich rewards of your path unfold.

Your life is calling you toward all that you were created to be. Are you listening?

About the Author

VALORIE BURTON is a sought-after life coach and speaker whose daily radio feature *The Good Life* airs on stations nationwide. She is the author of *Rich Minds, Rich Rewards* and founder of Inspire, Inc., a life-enrichment company through which she inspires and empowers individuals to live fulfilling lives. A frequent media contributor, Valorie has engaged in more than two hundred inspiring radio and television interviews, appearing on CNN, UPN, TBN, BET, The Word Network, and on local affiliates of NBC, ABC, CBS, Fox, WB, and NPR. She served as a monthly columnist and contributing editor for *Heart & Soul Magazine* and as cohost with T. D. Jakes of the national daily television program *The Potter's Touch*. She is also a columnist for BlackAmericaWeb.com.

She earned a master's degree in journalism from Florida A&M University and graduated from Florida State University with a bachelor's degree in International Affairs. Valorie and her husband live in the Washington, D.C., area.